THE
CHOCTAW

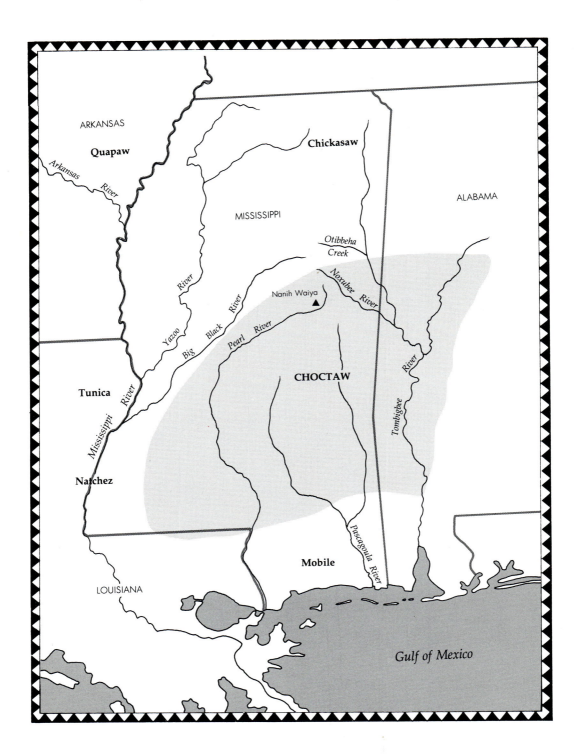

THE
CHOCTAW

Jesse O. McKee
University of Southern Mississippi

Frank W. Porter III
General Editor

CHELSEA HOUSE PUBLISHERS
New York   Philadelphia

On the cover Fabric dolls made in 1880 representing a Choctaw woman (left) and man (right) in clothing of the period.

Chelsea House Publishers
Editor-in-Chief   Nancy Toff
Executive Editor   Remmel T. Nunn
Managing Editor   Karyn Gullen Browne
Copy Chief   Juliann Barbato
Picture Editor   Adrian G. Allen
Art Director   Maria Epes
Manufacturing Manager   Gerald Levine

Indians of North America
Senior Editor   Marjorie P. K. Weiser

Staff for **THE CHOCTAW**
Associate Editor   Liz Sonneborn
Deputy Copy Chief   Ellen Scordato
Editorial Assistant   Claire Wilson
Assistant Art Director   Laurie Jewell
Designer   Donna Sinisgalli
Design Assistant   James Baker
Picture Researcher   Andrea Reithmayr
Production Coordinator   Joseph Romano

7   9   8

Library of Congress Cataloging-in-Publication Data

McKee, Jesse O.
The Choctaw.
(Indians of North America)
Bibliography: p.
Includes index.
Summary: Examines the history, culture, and changing fortunes of the Choctaw Indians.
1. Choctaw Indians. [1. Choctaw Indians. 2. Indians of North America] I. Title. II. Series: Indians of North America (Chelsea House Publishers)
E99.C8M36   1989   973′.0497   88-30165
ISBN   1-55546-699-0
        0-7910-0375-2 (pbk.)

CONTENTS

INDIANS OF NORTH AMERICA

CHELSEA HOUSE PUBLISHERS

INDIANS OF NORTH AMERICA: CONFLICT AND SURVIVAL

Frank W. Porter III

The Indians survived our open intention of wiping them out, and since the tide turned they have even weathered our good intentions toward them, which can be much more deadly.

John Steinbeck
America and Americans

When Europeans first reached the North American continent, they found hundreds of tribes occupying a vast and rich country. The newcomers quickly recognized the wealth of natural resources. They were not, however, so quick or willing to recognize the spiritual, cultural, and intellectual riches of the people they called Indians.

The Indians of North America examines the problems that develop when people with different cultures come together. For American Indians, the consequences of their interaction with non-Indian people have been both productive and tragic. The Europeans believed they had "discovered" a "New World," but their religious bigotry, cultural bias, and materialistic world view kept them from appreciating and understanding the people who lived in it. All too often they attempted to change the way of life of the indigenous people. The Spanish conquistadores wanted the Indians as a source of labor. The Christian missionaries, many of whom were English, viewed them as potential converts. French traders and trappers used the Indians as a means to obtain pelts. As Francis Parkman, the 19th-century historian, stated, "Spanish civilization crushed the Indian; English civilization scorned and neglected him; French civilization embraced and cherished him."

Nearly 500 years later, many people think of American Indians as curious vestiges of a distant past, waging a futile war to survive in a Space Age society. Even today, our understanding of the history and culture of American Indians is too often derived from unsympathetic, culturally biased, and inaccurate reports. The American Indian, described and portrayed in thousands of movies, television programs, books, articles, and government studies, has either been raised to the status of the "noble savage" or disparaged as the "wild Indian" who resisted the westward expansion of the American frontier.

7

Where in this popular view are the real Indians, the human beings and communities whose ancestors can be traced back to ice-age hunters? Where are the creative and indomitable people whose sophisticated technologies used the natural resources to ensure their survival, whose military skill might even have prevented European settlement of North America if not for devastating epidemics and the disruption of the ecology? Where are the men and women who are today diligently struggling to assert their legal rights and express once again the value of their heritage?

The various Indian tribes of North America, like people everywhere, have a history that includes population expansion, adaptation to a range of regional environments, trade across wide networks, internal strife, and warfare. This was the reality. Europeans justified their conquests, however, by creating a mythical image of the New World and its native people. In this myth, the New World was a virgin land, waiting for the Europeans. The arrival of Christopher Columbus ended a timeless primitiveness for the original inhabitants.

Also part of this myth was the debate over the origins of the American Indians. Fantastic and diverse answers were proposed by the early explorers, missionaries, and settlers. Some thought that the Indians were descended from the Ten Lost Tribes of Israel, others that they were descended from inhabitants of the lost continent of Atlantis. One writer suggested that the Indians had reached North America in another Noah's ark.

A later myth, perpetrated by many historians, focused on the relentless persecution during the past five centuries until only a scattering of these "primitive" people remained to be herded onto reservations. This view fails to chronicle the overt and covert ways in which the Indians successfully coped with the intruders.

All of these myths presented one-sided interpretations that ignored the complexity of European and American events and policies. All left serious questions unanswered. What were the origins of the American Indians? Where did they come from? How and when did they get to the New World? What was their life—their culture—really like?

In the late 1800s, anthropologists and archaeologists in the Smithsonian Institution's newly created Bureau of American Ethnology in Washington, D. C., began to study scientifically the history and culture of the Indians of North America. They were motivated by an honest belief that the Indians were on the verge of extinction and that along with them would vanish their languages, religious beliefs, technology, myths, and legends. These men and women went out to visit, study, and record data from as many Indian communities as possible before this information was forever lost.

By this time there was a new myth in the national consciousness. American Indians existed as figures in the American past. They had performed a historical mission. They had challenged white settlers who trekked across the continent. Once conquered, however, they were supposed to accept graciously the way of life of their conquerors.

The reality again was different. American Indians resisted both actively and passively. They refused to lose their unique identity, to be assimilated into white society. Many whites viewed the Indians not only as members of a conquered nation but also as "inferior" and "unequal." The rights of the Indians could be expanded, contracted, or modified as the conquerors saw fit. In every generation, white society asked itself what to do with the American Indians. Their answers have resulted in the twists and turns of federal Indian policy.

There were two general approaches. One way was to raise the Indians to a "higher level" by "civilizing" them. Zealous missionaries considered it their Christian duty to elevate the Indian through conversion and scanty education. The other approach was to ignore the Indians until they disappeared under pressure from the ever-expanding white society. The myth of the "vanishing Indian" gave stronger support to the latter option, helping to justify the taking of the Indians' land.

Prior to the end of the 18th century, there was no national policy on Indians simply because the American nation had not yet come into existence. American Indians similarly did not possess a political or social unity with which to confront the various Europeans. They were not homogeneous. Rather, they were loosely formed bands and tribes, speaking nearly 300 languages and thousands of dialects. The collective identity felt by Indians today is a result of their common experiences of defeat and/or mistreatment at the hands of whites.

During the colonial period, the British crown did not have a coordinated policy toward the Indians of North America. Specific tribes (most notably the Iroquois and the Cherokee) became military and political pawns used by both the crown and the individual colonies. The success of the American Revolution brought no immediate change. When the United States acquired new territory from France and Mexico in the early 19th century, the federal government wanted to open this land to settlement by homesteaders. But the Indian tribes that lived on this land had signed treaties with European governments assuring their title to the land. Now the United States assumed legal responsibility for honoring these treaties.

At first, President Thomas Jefferson believed that the Louisiana Purchase contained sufficient land for both the Indians and the white population.

Within a generation, though, it became clear that the Indians would not be allowed to remain. In the 1830s the federal government began to coerce the eastern tribes to sign treaties agreeing to relinquish their ancestral land and move west of the Mississippi River. Whenever these negotiations failed, President Andrew Jackson used the military to remove the Indians. The southeastern tribes, promised food and transportation during their removal to the West, were instead forced to walk the "Trail of Tears." More than 4,000 men, women, and children died during this forced march. The "removal policy" was successful in opening the land to homesteaders, but it created enormous hardships for the Indians.

By 1871 most of the tribes in the United States had signed treaties ceding most or all of their ancestral land in exchange for reservations and welfare. The treaty terms were intended to bind both parties for all time. But in the General Allotment Act of 1887, the federal government changed its policy again. Now the goal was to make tribal members into individual landowners and farmers, encouraging their absorption into white society. This policy was advantageous to whites who were eager to acquire Indian land, but it proved disastrous for the Indians. One hundred thirty-eight million acres of reservation land were subdivided into tracts of 160, 80, or as little as 40 acres, and allotted to tribe members on an individual basis. Land owned in this way was said to have "trust status" and could not be sold. But the surplus land—all Indian land not allotted to individuals— was opened (for sale) to white settlers. Ultimately, more than 90 million acres of land were taken from the Indians by legal and illegal means.

The resulting loss of land was a catastrophe for the Indians. It was necessary to make it illegal for Indians to sell their land to non-Indians. The Indian Reorganization Act of 1934 officially ended the allotment period. Tribes that voted to accept the provisions of this act were reorganized, and an effort was made to purchase land within preexisting reservations to restore an adequate land base.

Ten years later, in 1944, federal Indian policy again shifted. Now the federal government wanted to get out of the "Indian business." In 1953 an act of Congress named specific tribes whose trust status was to be ended "at the earliest possible time." This new law enabled the United States to end unilaterally, whether the Indians wished it or not, the special status that protected the land in Indian tribal reservations. In the 1950s federal Indian policy was to transfer federal responsibility and jurisdiction to state governments, encourage the physical relocation of Indian peoples from reservations to urban areas, and hasten the termination, or extinction, of tribes.

Between 1954 and 1962 Congress passed specific laws authorizing the termination of more than 100 tribal groups. The stated purpose of the termination policy was to ensure the full and complete integration of Indians into American society. However, there is a less benign way to interpret this legislation. Even as termination was being discussed in Congress, 133 separate bills were introduced to permit the transfer of trust land ownership from Indians to non-Indians.

With the Johnson administration in the 1960s the federal government began to reject termination. In the 1970s yet another Indian policy emerged. Known as "self-determination," it favored keeping the protective role of the federal government while increasing tribal participation in, and control of, important areas of local government. In 1983 President Reagan, in a policy statement on Indian affairs, restated the unique "government to government" relationship of the United States with the Indians. However, federal programs since then have moved toward transferring Indian affairs to individual states, which have long desired to gain control of Indian land and resources.

As long as American Indians retain power, land, and resources that are coveted by the states and the federal government, there will continue to be a "clash of cultures," and the issues will be contested in the courts, Congress, the White House, and even in the international human rights community. To give all Americans a greater comprehension of the issues and conflicts involving American Indians today is a major goal of this series. These issues are not easily understood, nor can these conflicts be readily resolved. The study of North American Indian history and culture is a necessary and important step toward that comprehension. All Americans must learn the history of the relations between the Indians and the federal government, recognize the unique legal status of the Indians, and understand the heritage and cultures of the Indians of North America.

Nanih Waiya, the sacred mound in the center of the Choctaw ancestral homeland.

CHOCTAW ORIGINS

The Choctaw are great storytellers. They have two stories of their origin, which they have passed on orally from generation to generation for many centuries. One maintains that the Choctaw first lived somewhere in what is now the western United States and then migrated to present-day Mississippi. Although the story does not fully explain why the tribe left the West, some versions of it suggest that either their first homeland had become overpopulated or they wished to escape constant warfare with neighboring tribes. Carrying the bones of their ancestors, the Choctaw journeyed eastward, a course indicated by a sacred pole that their leader, Chata, placed in the ground at the end of each day's journey. Every morning, they found the pole was leaning toward the east and set off in that direction, led by a white dog with magical powers that slept at the base of the pole each night. For months the Choctaw wandered, crossing a great river (the Mississippi) and continuing east.

Finally, one morning, they found that the dog had died and that the pole stood upright. The Choctaw took this as a sign that they had at last arrived in their new homeland.

To celebrate the occasion, the Choctaw built a large mound in which they buried their ancestors' remains. Because the mound was slanted, they called it *Nanih Waiya*, or "leaning mound." This great oblong structure, located in what is today southern Winston County in east-central Mississippi, stood nearly 40 feet high with a base of approximately one acre and a summit of about one-fourth of an acre. The Choctaw fortified the mound with an eight-foot-high circular wall measuring one and a half to two miles in circumference. Archaeologists believe that the mound was the location for political and religious meetings of the tribe from about 500 B.C. until the arrival of Europeans in the area in the early 1700s.

The Choctaw's second story of their origin states that they were created in the center of Nanih Waiya by a great spirit and then crawled to the surface of the earth through a hole in the ground or a cave. In another version of this creation story, the Creek, Cherokee, and Chickasaw Indians came out of the mound before the Choctaw finally emerged. The other groups migrated to neighboring areas, but when the Choctaw surfaced, they dried themselves in the sun, looked around, and chose to settle on the land surrounding Nanih Waiya.

The early Choctaw left no written records of the way they lived, but archaeologists and other scholars have learned much about the Choctaw's prehistory from studying artifacts—handmade objects they left behind, such as projectile points (arrowheads or spear points) and pottery. The written observations of the European explorers and

The Mississippi River, as seen from an overlook near the present-day city of Natchez, Mississippi. Choctaw legend holds that long ago the tribe crossed the river as it traveled eastward in search of a new home.

travelers who visited the area as early as the 16th century also contribute information about prehistoric Choctaw life.

The region the early Choctaw inhabited (now Mississippi, western Alabama, and eastern Louisiana) has a warm, moist climate with mild winters, hot summers, and ample rainfall. The area is covered with low, rolling hills blanketed with pine trees, and hardwoods are found along the many creeks and rivers that flow through the land. The forests provided the Choctaw with firewood and building materials, and the wild plants, game, and fish, abundant in the region, provided much of their food.

Although the soil was not extremely rich, Choctaw men, women, and children cultivated the river floodplains. All Choctaw land was held in common by the tribe, but individuals had a claim to any tract they cultivated as long as they did not encroach upon fields already claimed by other Choctaw. If a Choctaw abandoned his or her field, control over it reverted to the tribe.

The Choctaw cleared their fields in midwinter by burning the underbrush and killing the trees by cutting off a ring of bark near the base of their trunks. In the spring, they planted corn (maize)—their most important crop—beans, melons, pumpkins, peas, squash, sweet potatoes, and sunflowers. The tribe's farming tools included spades and shovels made from cedarwood and hoes constructed from pieces of flint, the bones of an animal, such as the

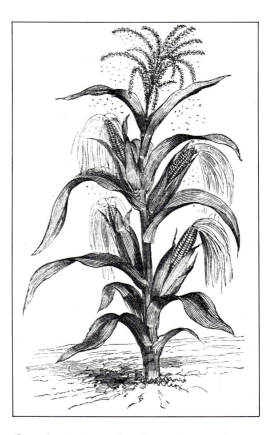

Corn (maize) was the Choctaw's most important crop and the main ingredient in many traditional dishes.

shoulder blades of a bison, or bent sticks.

When the men were not working in the fields, they fished and hunted wild game, which provided the Choctaw with much of their food. Hunting parties stalked deer, bear, bison, turkey, squirrel, otter, beaver, raccoon, and rabbit and killed their prey with bows and arrows, axes, knives, and tomahawks. Aside from being the tribe's main meat source, deer and bears gave

A bow and arrow used by the early Choctaw to kill fish. Other methods for catching fish included dragging nets made from brush along river bottoms and poisoning the animals with juice from berries or buckeyes.

the Choctaw skins, which they made into clothing and moccasins. They also created ornaments and necklaces from bear claws and from bone fragments of other animals, and they cooked their food and groomed their hair and body with oil found in bear fat.

Boys, and sometimes girls, joined hunting expeditions close to the fields. Early in life, they were taught to recognize the tracks of small animals, which they hunted with blowguns made of seven-foot-long reeds. After loading an arrowhead into the reed,

children would aim it at their prey and then project the arrowhead by blowing into the pipe. As boys grew older, their male elders taught them good sportsmanship and hunting skills, such as how to track and locate larger animals and how to use the bow and arrow. Men also trained boys for bow-and-arrow competitions, which were popular with the Choctaw.

Children, women, and the elderly added to the food supply by gathering wild plants, fruits, and nuts in tall grass baskets. Hickory nuts, pecans, walnuts, chestnuts, and acorns were especially important to the tribe. Women, who were responsible for all food preparation, often mixed nuts with water, combined them with vegetables or breads, or used them for stews, oil, and drinks.

The main ingredient of many of the Choctaw's favorite dishes was corn, which they used to make grits, hominy, porridge, and meal. Choctaw women also pounded boiled corn (*tafula*) and frequently mixed it with beans. Another popular dish, *bunaha*, consisted of pounded cornmeal combined with boiled beans. The Choctaw wrapped this dough in corn husks, then boiled the husks, and set them aside until they needed the cooked bunaha.

The Choctaw paid a great deal of attention to their clothing and ornaments. Men always wore a belt and a loincloth. In the winter they also put on leggings and moccasins and wore garments woven from feathers or the bark of mulberry trees on their upper torsos.

Women wore short skirts of deerskin, but when the weather was cold, they also wrapped themselves in deerskin shawls and put on moccasins. Both men and women often wore brightly colored ornaments made from nuts, bones, stones, and seeds and sometimes placed feathers in their hair.

The early Choctaw built their homes with a wood frame made of posts fastened together with vines. They plastered the interior with mud, which dried in the sun to form windowless walls. The Choctaw then covered the outside with the bark of cypress or pine trees. The single door was only about three to four feet high. Because the Choctaw built fires in the middle of their dwellings for heat and cooking, they left a hole at the top of two opposite walls to let the smoke out. The most used furnishings in their homes were platforms woven from cane, which served as beds, tables, and seats. Skins of bears, deer, or bison (buffalo) were used for blankets, and sun-baked earthen pots and pans, for cooking.

Most Choctaw lived in villages, which were located within three geographic divisions: *Okla Falaya* (long people), to the northwest; *Okla Tannap*, or *Ahepat Okla* (people of the opposite side), to the northeast; and *Okla Hannali* (people of Six Towns), to the south. For most of their prehistory, the Choctaw probably lived in just these three districts, but there may have once been a small, fourth division, called *Okla Chito* (big people), in the center of the Choctaw domain.

Each of the three divisions grew up around one of their land's three major rivers—the Pearl, the Tombigbee, and the Pascagoula, respectively—and its tributaries. There were slight variations in the dress and speech among the inhabitants of the three divisions, but more significant were the different alliances and trade relations between each division and the neighboring tribes geographically closest to it. Okla Falaya had strong ties to the Chakchiuma and Chickasaw to the west; Okla Tannap, to the Alabama to the east; and Okla Hannali, to smaller Indian groups, such as the Mobile, to the south.

Each geographic division was governed by a *mingo* or district chief. A mingo was elected by the men within his district and was usually a man from an influential family with demonstrated leadership ability. Each village also had

This wooden spoon was carved more than 300 years ago. The Choctaw also made spoons and dishes from buffalo horns.

its own chief to preside over meetings of a council composed of village elders. Village chiefs were aided by four or five assistants, who often helped them to predict the future. One of the assistants was a war chief in charge of all military matters.

When it was necessary, a mingo would call for a council of all village chiefs in his division. The three district chiefs, who together governed the affairs of the entire tribal nation, sometimes called for a national council composed of the members of all three district councils. Council decisions had to be supported by a majority of the meeting's participants. Thus, with its election of officials, civilian rule, and unlimited opportunity for issues to be debated, the Choctaw system of government was in many respects very democratic.

Socially, the Choctaw were separated into two divisions, each of which contained six to eight clans. Division membership had great significance. For instance, marriage between members of the same division or the same clan was prohibited. Because the Choctaw were matrilineal, meaning that they traced descent through the female side of the family, children belonged to their mother's clan, while their father was a member of the clan of his own mother. If parents were separated, the offspring always remained with the mother.

Choctaw children were raised in an atmosphere of relative freedom. A mother was responsible for the upbringing of her daughters. A mother's

brothers, however, took charge of that of her sons because they were the boys' closest male relatives who were members of the children's clan. Maternal uncles disciplined and trained boys in hunting, warfare, and ball playing. If a boy was disobedient, an older man often punished him, first with a scolding and then by pouring cold water on the boy.

Children were frequently named after some event that occurred at the time they were born. Later in life, a Choctaw was given another name as a result of some adventure, exploit, or personal characteristic. A speech or a ceremony sometimes accompanied the granting of this second name.

Although the early Choctaw conducted few ceremonies, singing and dancing were a part of their everyday life, and they held feasts regularly. Among the most important dances the Choctaw performed were the green corn dance, held in the late summer in anticipation of the corn harvest; the war dance, before military expeditions; and the ball-play dance, on nights before the Choctaw played *ishtaboli*, the tribe's favorite ball game. They held other less significant dances to honor various birds and animals, such as the turkey, bison, and bear. The Choctaw usually performed these dances in an open space in the center of each village to the beat of a drum. To make a drum, a Choctaw would cut a section from the trunk of a small hollow tree and stretch a fresh deerskin over the opening. When the skin dried, it became tight.

They then played the instrument by hitting it with a stick.

One of the recreational activities the Choctaw enjoyed most was playing ishtaboli, a ball game similar to the one that we know today as lacrosse. At the start of the game, the players, divided into two teams, would gather at the center of a large field with goals at each end. A judge would then toss into the air a small leather ball, which the players would chase, trying to hit it across the field with their two rackets, called *kapuchas*. The objective was to hit the ball into the goal of the player's team. The game was over when one team had scored a set number of goals, usually 10 or 20.

Ishtaboli was a social event involving men and women, young and old. Most games were played between different villages or against a neighboring tribe, usually with 75–100 players to a team. Although the Choctaw followed complicated rules of play and etiquette, it was a bruising and vicious game. Players often suffered broken bones when they were hit or tackled.

The Choctaw believed in spiritual entities, but they probably did not worship a single supreme being. However, they did consider the sun to be a particularly powerful force. The Choctaw also thought that some members of their society possessed special powers and often consulted these enchanters, healers, rainmakers, and prophets. Their *alikchi*, or medicine men, used their powers to predict future events, help hunters to be successful in the

A tail of horsehair, which Choctaw men wore while playing ishtaboli. They tucked the hook into the back of their loincloth and then strapped a belt around their waist to hold the tail in place.

chase, or instill bravery in warriors. Some were skilled in treating wounds and diagnosing diseases and knew of many plants and other antidotes that could cure various illnesses. Other alikchi called on supernatural forces for evil purposes.

The Choctaw believed that every person had two souls that survived after death. These souls were not purely spiritual but took the form of a *shilup*, a ghost in the shape of a human. Upon death, one shilup, the "outside shadow," remained in the Choctaw homeland to frighten the living. The other, the "inside shadow," went to one of two afterworlds. Both were located on earth a great distance away. After death, most Choctaw traveled to the good afterworld, a pleasant, sunny land, with plenty of animals for good hunting. Tribespeople who had committed murder, however, went to the bad afterworld, a cloudy and rainy place, with few animals to hunt. Its inhabitants were destined to an eternity of misery and discomfort.

When a Choctaw died, the corpse was wrapped in animal skin or tree bark and placed on a scaffold five or six feet from the ground. Friends and relatives visited the scaffold to cry, mourn, and

Two kapuchas (or ishtaboli rackets). Using a kapucha, a player caught the ball and whipped it through the air to a teammate or into the goal.

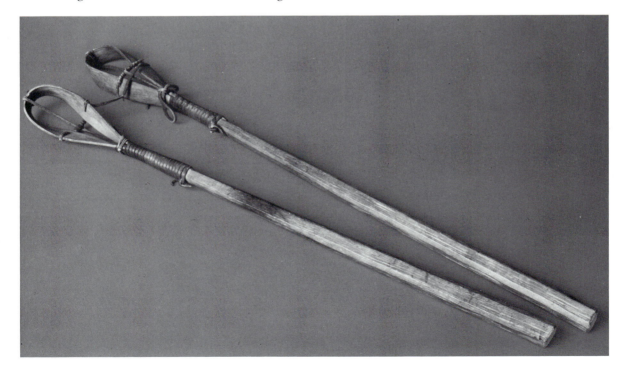

wail. When the body had decomposed, a painted and tattooed tribal official, known as a bone picker, would scrape off any remaining flesh from the bones with his long fingernails as the bereaved watched. The scaffold was then burned, and the bones were placed in a box, which was stored in a community bone house. Once the ceremony was over, the bone picker presided over a feast. Several times a year, when the bone house became full, the bones were removed and buried in a mound. A communal funeral attended by everyone in the village was then performed.

Perhaps the most distinguishing trait of the prehistoric Choctaw was the tribe's peaceful demeanor. The tribespeople almost never initiated warfare against their Indian neighbors, although they vigorously defended themselves whenever their lands were invaded. The practicality and adaptability that helped the early Choctaw avoid conflict also allowed them to develop their well-ordered social and political systems and healthy agricultural economy. These qualities would be severely tested, however, when Europeans first arrived in the land of the Choctaw in the mid-16th century. Despite the tribe's inclination, the Choctaw were to learn that war with these invaders could not always be avoided and that the price of preventing conflict with them would always be great. ▲

Choctaw Indians drawn by French artist Alexandre De Batz in the 1730s. The man is dressed and painted for war and carries a scalp on his staff.

2

EUROPEANS
AND
CHANGING WAYS

By late 1540, Choctaw district chief Tuscaloosa knew that Hernando de Soto was coming. The Spanish explorer and his men had landed in North America near what is today Tampa Bay in Florida more than a year earlier. Tuscaloosa had heard reports that the Spaniards were traveling northwest into the continent, pillaging entire villages on their way. They usually demanded food and other goods from the Indians they encountered and often enslaved them to work as servants and baggage carriers. Because the Spaniards seldom stayed in one location for any length of time, Tuscaloosa hoped to be able to extend hospitality to de Soto and his soldiers, meet their minimum requests, and then quickly see them on their way.

De Soto arrived in Tuscaloosa's village in the eastern portion of the Choctaw domain early in October 1540. The first meeting between the explorer and the chief was cordial. They ate together,

and later the Choctaw performed a dance. The following day, de Soto demanded carriers, canoes, and women. Tuscaloosa gave de Soto some Choctaw carriers, built the Spaniards rafts, because the Choctaw had no canoes, and promised to supply the soldiers with women when the Europeans reached the Choctaw village of Mabila (near the present-day city of Mobile, Alabama). Tuscaloosa secretly sent a message to the chief of Mabila, warning him of the approaching Spaniards and cautioning him to be prepared to defend his town should the need arise.

Forcing Tuscaloosa and several of his assistants to join them, the Spaniards soon departed for Mabila. When the party arrived there on October 18, 1540, it was greeted by the tribespeople with dances, songs, and chants. Tuscaloosa then presented de Soto with a gift, and reminding de Soto that his demands had been met, the chief requested his own release. When de Soto hesitated, Tuscaloosa walked away, entered a dwelling that was surrounded by many Choctaw armed with bows and arrows, and refused to come out. Inspired by his act of defiance, the Choctaw then attacked de Soto and his men, driving the Spaniards out of the village. The tribespeople unchained the men who had been enslaved and seized the Spaniards' baggage, which the carriers had placed inside the palisade (village wall) before the battle began. Among the spoils were 200 pounds of pearls, Christian sacramental vessels, food, wine, clothing, and some arms and ammunition.

Outside the palisade, de Soto and his men regrouped and prepared to attack Mabila. In the battle that followed, the Choctaw's bows and arrows, which could not penetrate the European soldiers' armor, proved no match for the Spaniards' firearms and lances. The Spaniards regained entrance into the village and set the stockade and several houses on fire. Many Choctaw were killed in the bloody battle, and some died in the fire. Several of the tribespeople who survived hanged themselves from trees with their bowstrings rather than fall as prisoners to the Spaniards. As many as 1,500 Choctaw men, women, and children, including Tuscaloosa, lost their lives. Spanish casualties were estimated at only 22 dead and 148 wounded.

De Soto remained in Mabila until his wounded men had healed and his soldiers had seized enough corn and other supplies to continue their journey. On November 14, 1540, de Soto and more than 500 men finally left the village. They headed northwest and eventually crossed from the eastern portion of the Choctaw homeland into the land of the Chickasaw Indians, where they became the first Europeans to see the Mississippi River.

Following the departure of de Soto, the Choctaw did not have any sustained contact with Europeans for 150 years, although foreign explorers and settlers continued to travel to North America. The Spanish claimed vast areas of land in present-day Florida, Mexico, and the western United States; the English built colonies along the Atlantic Coast; and the French explored much of Canada and the Mississippi River valley. But because very few of these Europeans came to live on the Choctaw's lands, the tribe continued to live for the next century and a half in much the same way it had before their first disastrous encounter with white men.

Not until the beginning of the 18th century did Europeans start to exert an influence over the Indians in what is now the southeastern United States. The Spanish had the least authority in the area because of the small population of their settlements, although Spanish missionaries and traders in Pensacola (in present-day northwestern Florida) had contact with the neighboring Indian tribes. English settlers, especially those in the highly populated colony of Carolina (now portions of North Carolina, South Carolina, and Georgia), had much more contact with inland Indians. Trade with these tribes was one of their primary economic activities.

The French had become the dominant European presence in the lower Mississippi valley and therefore were to have the greatest influence on the Choctaw. In the late 17th century, Louis Jolliet and Jacques Marquette, and later Robert Cavelier, Sieur de La Salle, had explored much of the Mississippi River. Under the leadership of Pierre Le Moyne, Sieur d'Iberville, the French es-

tablished a permanent settlement at Fort Maurepas, on the coast of the Gulf of Mexico near old Biloxi (now Ocean Springs), in 1699. More French settlements soon followed: Mobile, located on the Gulf Coast in 1702; Fort Rosalie, at Natchez on the Mississippi River, in 1716; New Orleans, at the mouth of the river, in 1718; and Fort St. Pierre, at Yazoo, north of Natchez on the Yazoo River, in 1719.

As more and more Europeans came to North America, the competition be-

The Choctaw fighting Hernando de Soto and his soldiers at the Battle of Mabila. The chroniclers of de Soto's expedition describe the Choctaw's terror at the sight of the Spaniards on horseback. The Indians had never seen horses before and feared that these unfamiliar animals were supernatural beings.

tween England, Spain, and France for dominance on the continent heightened. So did their desire for military and trade alliances with the Indians. The English particularly relied on trade with the Indians, because slaves had become vital to the economy of the English colonies. The colonists imported African slaves to work as field hands, carpenters, blacksmiths, and mechanics, but they also traded guns, ammunition, knives, axes, hoes, and cooking utensils to some Indians in exchange for Indian slaves they captured from other tribes. There were many Indian slaves in Carolina, but others were sent to New England or the West Indies. Besides trade, it was important for all three powers to gain Indian military support in order to strengthen their own position and guard their claims on the continent against their European rivals. Therefore, much of the history of the 18th century in North America involves the conflict between the European settlers and their struggle for power and advantage over each other. For the Indians, this struggle often

A French map showing animal life along the Mississippi River in 1740. The Choctaw homeland is labeled Pays des Chactas (land of the Choctaw).

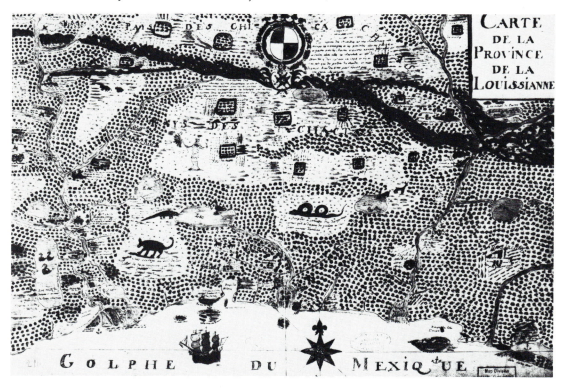

meant almost continual warfare, because each European power encouraged its Indian allies to battle its European rivals and their respective Indian allies.

With the French to their west and the English to their east, the Choctaw held a strategic position that caused both colonial powers to seek their allegiance. The tribe almost always preferred the French, initially because their presence on the Mississippi made them the most available trading partners and because the French governors had given gifts to the Choctaw chiefs from the start of their contact. The Choctaw, however, soon came to see the English as their own enemies after the English-allied Chickasaw Indians to the north began raiding Choctaw villages as well as those of neighboring tribes, such as the Taena and the Tunica, and taking Indian slaves. The Choctaw and the Chickasaw had been warring for several years when Choctaw leaders met with the French at old Biloxi in 1699 to discuss their mutual dislike of the English. Seeing an opportunity to hurt their European rival, the French agreed to aid the Choctaw in their battles against the English and the Chickasaw.

The Choctaw-Chickasaw conflict continued until French colonial leader d'Iberville invited representatives of several area tribes to meet with him at a council in Mobile in 1702. D'Iberville persuaded the Chickasaw to become the allies of the French and the Choctaw. This peace lasted less than two

French explorer and diplomat Pierre Le Moyne, Sieur d'Iberville.

years. Enraged that the Chickasaw had resumed their trading relations with the English, again providing them with goods and slaves, the Choctaw attacked the Chickasaw in 1703, and the war between the tribes resumed. Another peace was made in 1708, but fighting began again in 1711, when the Creek and Chickasaw, with English backing, invaded the Choctaw homeland and inflicted heavy casualties. After this successful campaign by the English, the Choctaw became their allies. Not surprisingly, this shift in allegiance was short lived. By 1715, the Choctaw were back with the French, and by 1720, the French and Choctaw were again at war with the Chickasaw, a conflict that lasted for the next five years.

By the end of the 1720s, the French were also in conflict with the Natchez Indians, who lived along the Mississippi River near the present-day city of Natchez, Mississippi. Relations between the French and the Natchez had once been good, but the Natchez became hostile as French settlers began to take control of more and more of their fertile land on the river. Possibly encouraged by the Chickasaw and the English, the tribe began a series of attacks on French settlements. The most violent occurred in 1729, when the Natchez stormed Fort Rosalie, which the Indians themselves had built for the French 13 years earlier. The Natchez slaughtered 250 soldiers, took nearly 300 women and children prisoner, and almost destroyed the fort. With the aid of the Choctaw, the enraged French struck back in 1730 and rescued their prisoners. By 1731, they had practically annihilated the entire Natchez tribe. The survivors came to live with the Chickasaw and the Cherokee or were captured and sold into slavery, usually in the West Indies.

After nearly 50 years of constant warfare and shifting allegiances, the Choctaw began to fight among themselves. Okla Falaya had become sympathetic to the English, Okla Tannap remained loyal to the French, and Okla Hannali was divided. The two factions grew so unfriendly that a civil war broke out in the tribe in 1748, resulting in heavy losses to both sides. Soon, French leader Carlos de Grandpré intervened and with a detachment of French soldiers helped defeat the pro-English Choctaw faction. In 1750, peace was established with the Grandpré Treaty, in which the French imposed some harsh controls on the Choctaw people. The treaty stated that any Choctaw who killed a Frenchman or invited an Englishman to a Choctaw village would be put to death. It also provided that the Choctaw would continue to battle the Chickasaw and "never cease to strike at that perfidious race as long as there should be any portion of it remaining."

The Grandpré Treaty helped fuel the Choctaw's growing disillusionment with their French allies. In 1754, angry because the French had stopped their regular distribution of gifts to the tribe, the Choctaw threatened to enter into an allegiance with the English. Their demands received little attention, however, because the French were occupied with battling the English in the French and Indian War, which had erupted to the east in the same year. This final war between these powers for supremacy in North America ended in 1763 with the signing of the Treaty of Paris. England agreed to return Cuba to Spain in ex-

Fort Rosalie on the Mississippi, the site of a massacre of French settlers by Natchez Indians in 1729.

change for Florida. The defeated French ceded Canada to the English, gave their lands west of the river (known as Louisiana) to the Spanish, and relinquished all claims to other territory east of the Mississippi. Thus French colonial ambitions in North America came to an end.

The English attempted to establish control over the territory between their settlements along the Atlantic coast and the Mississippi River by making treaties with various inland Indian groups, including the Choctaw, Chickasaw, Cherokee, and Creek. In 1765, the Choctaw met with British authorities in Mobile, where they signed a treaty that defined their eastern boundary approximately as the Alabama and Cahaba rivers and prohibited English settlers from moving into their land. While encamped there, the Choctaw were attacked by the Creek Indians, which led to a war that lasted for six years. Fearing the belligerent Creek, the English encouraged the Chickasaw and Cherokee to join the fighting on the side of the Choctaw.

The Choctaw's loyalties to the English were not strong, however. During the American Revolution (1776–83), some Choctaw served as scouts for the American armies as they battled British troops. The Americans emerged victorious, and with the Treaty of 1783, England surrendered her North American territory east of the Mississippi and south of Canada to the United States,

with the exception of East and West Florida, which it ceded to Spain. The Choctaw were not disappointed that their land was no longer under British control.

But nearly 80 years of contact with the English and the French had left their mark on the Choctaw. The intermarriage of Europeans and Choctaw particularly disrupted their traditional society by reducing the influence of the clan system and tribal customs. The increasing number of Choctaw of mixed ancestry also made it easier for the tribe to accept the values of non-Indian society.

Even more disturbing to the traditional Choctaw way of life were the consequences of the continual wars the tribe had waged at the insistence of its European allies. Before contact with Europeans, the Choctaw had been a non-

A Choctaw powder horn made in the 1770s. The elaborate carving was added in the 1860s by the owner at that time, Julius Folsom.

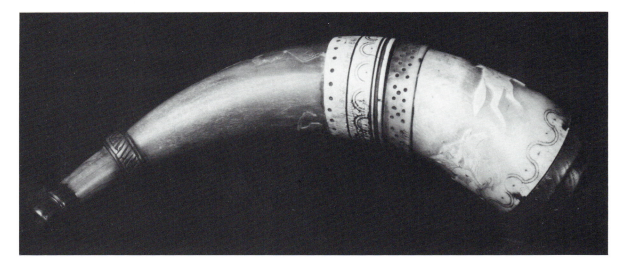

aggressive people, with no desire to expand their territory. But their allegiances, particularly with the French, led the Choctaw knowingly, although possibly unwillingly at times, to aid their European allies' attempts to extend their influence on the American continent. As a result, the Choctaw had been at war for most of the 18th century, battling among themselves as well as against neighboring tribes and colonial intruders. The few new European trade goods and diplomatic skills the Choctaw had acquired were a small consolation for the constant conflict and loss of Choctaw lives. Now under the control of the United States, the Choctaw would enter a period of increased contact with non-Indians, which would change their lives even more. ▲

Chief Pushmataha in an 1824 painting by C. B. King. During treaty negotiations in 1819, Pushmataha voiced his people's reluctance to remove to the West: "I am well acquainted with the country contemplated for us. I have often had my feet sorely bruised there by the roughness of its surface."

THE
LOSS
OF THE
HOMELAND

Immediately after the end of the American Revolution, the United States sought to gain dominance over the vast amount of land it had acquired under the terms of the Treaty of Paris. Because there were few American settlers in the southwestern portion of this territory, the United States was particularly concerned about gaining support from the many Indians in the South and reducing the possibility of hostilities with them. To strengthen its influence, the U.S. government began to enter into a series of treaties with the southern Indians.

On January 3, 1786, the Choctaw signed the Treaty of Hopewell, the first of nine agreements they would make with the U.S. government between 1786 and 1830. It established perpetual peace and friendship between the two parties, defined the eastern boundary of the Choctaw's territory as the same border described in the tribe's 1756 treaty with the English, gave the United States the right to build trading posts on Choctaw land, guaranteed the tribe the protection of the U.S. Army, and provided that any U.S. citizen living within the territory of the Choctaw was subject to tribal jurisdiction.

The Spanish were concerned by the Choctaw's friendly relationship with the new U.S. government. They feared that American settlers would soon move westward into the Choctaw domain and from there eventually into Spanish-owned lands west of the Mississippi. To protect their interests, the Spanish established forts on the western and eastern borders of Choctaw land. They first purchased a tract of land from the Choctaw and Chickasaw on the western edge of Choctaw territory and built Fort Nogales near the mouth of the Yazoo River. There the Spanish signed a treaty of friendship with the Choctaw, Chickasaw, Cherokee, and Creek in 1792. The Spanish also convinced the Choctaw to sell an-

Thomas Pinckney, the American diplomat for whom Pinckney's Treaty (the Treaty of San Lorenzo) was named.

other tract in the eastern section of their country near the Tombigbee River. The tribe was hesitant to part with this land, but the Spanish convinced the Indians that a Spanish fort in this location could protect them if the United States ever grew hostile. On this site, the Spanish constructed Fort Confederation.

The Spanish presence among the Choctaw did not last long. After the pro-Spanish Creek were defeated in a series of clashes with the U.S.-supplied Chickasaw, the United States and Spain, in 1795, signed the Treaty of San Lorenzo (also called Pinckney's Treaty, after U.S. major general Thomas Pinckney, who helped negotiate it). In the treaty, Spain agreed to remove her settlers from land north of the 31st parallel and was therefore forced to abandon Fort Nogales and Fort Confederation.

With the Spanish gone from the area, the United States was now able to form a program for dealing with the Choctaw and other southern tribes. The government soon began to send agents to work with the different Indian groups. These officials were responsible for enforcing federal laws within the tribal domains. Also at this time, the U.S. government began to organize politically the Indian country between the Mississippi River and the states located on the East Coast, anticipating that many white settlers would soon move west. In 1798, Mississippi Territory was formed from the southern portions of what are now Mississippi and Alabama. (The northern portions and the southern tips of these present-day states were added to Mississippi Territory in 1804 and 1812, respectively.)

The United States entered into its next two treaties with the Choctaw in order to buy portions of the tribe's territory for white settlers. With the Treaty of Fort Adams, signed on December 17, 1801, the government secured 2,264,920 acres of land in the southwest corner of the Choctaw's territory. It also secured the right to construct a road from the town of Natchez, on the Mississippi River, northeast across Choctaw country to Nashville, Tennessee. The Choctaw were compensated for the land with $2,000 in money and merchandise. The tribe was in desperate need of this

CHOCTAW LAND CESSIONS, 1801–1830

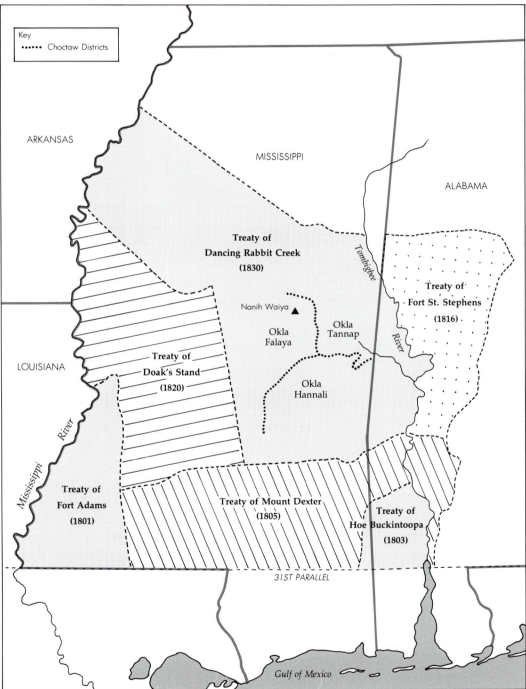

Key

•••• Choctaw Districts

ARKANSAS

MISSISSIPPI

ALABAMA

**Treaty of
Dancing Rabbit Creek**
(1830)

**Treaty of
Fort St. Stephens**
(1816)

Nanih Waiya ▲

Okla
Falaya

Okla
Tannap

LOUISIANA

**Treaty of
Doak's Stand**
(1820)

Okla
Hannali

Tombigbee

River

Mississippi

River

**Treaty of
Fort Adams**
(1801)

Treaty of Mount Dexter
(1805)

**Treaty of
Hoe Buckintoopa**
(1803)

31ST PARALLEL

Gulf of Mexico

payment because it was experiencing a famine owing to a drought that had nearly destroyed its crops the year before the signing of the treaty. The United States also provided three sets of blacksmith's tools for the Choctaw whose homes were located in the ceded land.

On October 7, 1802, the Choctaw signed the Treaty of Fort Confederation. This treaty redefined the Choctaw's eastern boundary, resulting in the tribe's cession of about 50,000 acres of land north of Mobile. Although the treaty granted the Choctaw only one dollar in compensation, they were willing to give up this relatively small tract of hunting land in order to preserve their friendly relationship with the U.S. government.

After these cessions, many Americans quickly settled around Natchez, on the Mississippi, and north of Mobile, in the lower Tombigbee River valley. To accommodate this influx of American settlers, President Thomas Jefferson assigned General James Wilkinson to discuss still another land cession with the Choctaw chiefs. General Wilkinson and the chiefs met at Hoe Buckintoopa, an Indian village near Mobile. The Choctaw initially refused to negotiate, but Wilkinson reminded the chiefs of debts the tribe owed to the British trading company of Panton, Leslie and Company, which was requesting immediate payment. The Choctaw reluctantly agreed to cede 853,760 acres of land north of Mobile if the U.S. government would pay their bill. The two parties signed the Treaty of Hoe Buckintoopa on August 31, 1803. In the treaty, the government compensated the chiefs by giving them each "15 pieces of stroud [woolen cloth], 3 rifles, 150 blankets, 250 rounds of powder, 250 pounds of lead, 1 bridle, 1 man's saddle, and 1 black silk handkerchief."

The liquidation of Choctaw debts in exchange for land was a ploy the U.S. government would use again in treaty negotiations with the Choctaw. In the Treaty of Mount Dexter (sometimes referred to as the First Choctaw Cession), signed on November 16, 1805, the Choctaw gave up 4,142,720 acres across the southern portion of the Choctaw territory. The Choctaw did not want to sign the treaty, but the government induced them to do so by offering to pay back another debt to Panton, Leslie and Company, this one amounting to $48,000. The U.S. government also agreed to give the tribe an annuity (annual payment) of $3,000, which the chiefs would be allowed to spend as they saw fit. In addition, each of the district chiefs was given a cash payment of $500 and a salary of $150 a year while he remained in this office. The treaty marked the beginning of the United States's payment of annuities to the Choctaw, which established a permanent tribal income and continued the custom of giving gifts to the chiefs in exchange for their cooperation.

During the years in which the United States negotiated these treaties with the Choctaw, Spain lost control of much of its land in North America. Although Spain did not officially cede Florida to the United States until 1819, it had progressively less authority over the region as more and more American settlers moved into it throughout the early 1800s. A more substantial loss was Louisiana, which Spain returned to France in 1800 because there were too few Spanish living in this vast territory to protect it from encroachment by other European settlers.

In 1803, the United States bought Louisiana from France, a purchase that almost doubled the country's area and moved its western border from the Mississippi River to the base of the Rocky Mountains. President Jefferson was anxious to use this land as a place to relocate (remove) Indians living east of the Mississippi and thereby open up more territory in the eastern United States for non-Indian settlers. Although it was several years before the U.S. government put this removal policy into action, Congress passed the Louisiana Territorial Act in 1804, giving the president the power to negotiate with Indian tribes for their removal.

The threat of removal and the continuing movement of Americans into lands inhabited by Indians inspired Tecumseh, leader of the Shawnee Indians of Delaware, to attempt to form an Indian confederacy. In 1811, Tecumseh and 30 warriors traveled south into Choctaw territory to elicit the tribe's support. After Tecumseh urged

U.S. general James Wilkinson, who negotiated the Treaty of Hoe Buckintoopa with the Choctaw in 1803.

the Choctaw's council to rise up against white intruders, Choctaw chief Pushmataha eloquently reminded the tribespeople of their long friendship with the United States. The council expelled Tecumseh, who then journeyed east into the land of the Creek, whom he found much more receptive to his message. In August 1813, a band of Creek Indians massacred the white inhabitants of Fort Mims in Alabama Territory, an attack that sparked a long war between that tribe and the United States. Hundreds of Choctaw and Chickasaw warriors joined the side of the U.S. Army in this

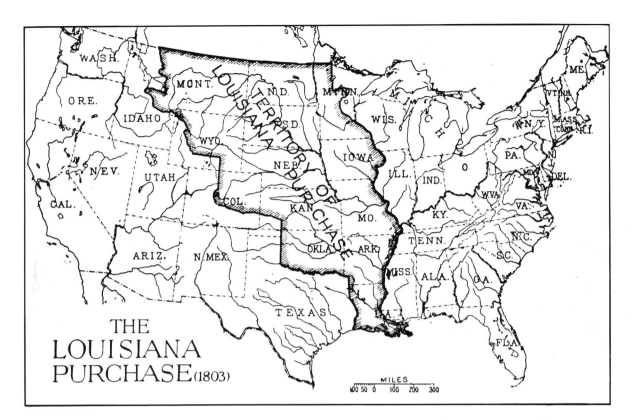

A 20th-century map showing the area bought by the United States in the Louisiana Purchase of 1803.

conflict. Many had already demonstrated their loyalty to the United States by fighting alongside American soldiers against the British during the War of 1812.

The Creek War created boundary disputes that the Choctaw chiefs and U.S. government officials met to settle in 1816 at the trading post at St. Stephens on the Tombigbee River. In the Treaty of Fort St. Stephens (also called the Treaty of 1816), signed on October 24, the Choctaw ceded approximately 3 million acres of land east of the Tom-

bigbee. The Choctaw were compensated with $10,000 in merchandise and a $6,000 annuity to be paid for 20 years. The parties agreed that the U.S. government would bank the annual payment but would give to the Choctaw the interest the money earned to establish and maintain Choctaw schools. The annual interest payment helped fund the first school in Choctaw territory, which was founded in 1818 at Elliot (near the present-day town of Grenada). Cyrus Kingsbury, a Presbyterian missionary and former Cherokee school instructor, set up the institution at the Choctaw's invitation.

In 1817, the western portion of Mississippi Territory became the state of Mississippi, and in 1819 the eastern portion became Alabama. This encouraged more and more whites to settle on the lands the Choctaw had ceded to the U.S. government. The population of the entire Mississippi Territory in 1800 was 8,850, but by 1820 the population of the state of Mississippi alone had grown to 75,448. Although the government tried to keep the newly arrived settlers and the Indians at peace, as the number of settlers increased, so did the pressure they exerted on the United States to acquire more land from the Indians and to remove entire tribes to western territory.

The United States tried to acquire additional Choctaw land in 1818 and 1819, but the tribe refused to cede any more territory. Finally, in October 1820, Generals Andrew Jackson and Thomas Hinds and Choctaw chiefs Pushmataha, Moshulatubbee, and Apukshunnubbee met at Doak's Stand, a grassy flat near the Pearl River in central Mississippi. After much discussion and argument, finally the Choctaw reluctantly signed the Treaty of Doak's Stand on October 18, 1820. The Choctaw thereby gave up 5,169,788 acres of their domain in exchange for approximately 13 million acres to the west. Most of the new

The Battle of New Orleans, one of several campaigns in which Choctaw soldiers joined American troops to fight the British during the War of 1812. This engraving is based on a sketch drawn by a major in the American army who witnessed the battle.

Reverend Cyrus Kingsbury, who founded Elliot, the first Choctaw school, in 1819.

land was in what is now Oklahoma and western Arkansas, between the Red River on the south and the Arkansas and Canadian rivers on the north—territory the U.S. government had acquired from the Quapaw Indians in 1818. In the treaty, Jackson also arranged for every Choctaw man to receive "a blanket, kettle, rifle gun, bullet molds and wipers, and ammunition sufficient for hunting and defense for one year plus enough corn . . . for one year."

After the treaty was signed, the United States expected the Choctaw to emigrate. The Choctaw's new land,

however, had not been fully surveyed, and its exact boundaries were not known. When the area was finally surveyed, the United States discovered that many white settlers were already living on the land owned by the Choctaw in what is now western Arkansas. The U.S. government decided a new treaty should be devised.

The Choctaw sent a delegation to Washington, D.C., in the late fall of 1824 to talk to representatives of the federal government about the problems stemming from the Treaty of Doak's Stand. Upon arrival, the Choctaw were wined and dined by U.S. officials, who believed negotiations would be easier if the Choctaw leaders were intoxicated by "firewater." The government's bar bill for the conference amounted to a staggering $2,149.50, with an additional $2,029 spent on food and lodgings for the Choctaw. Each delegate was also given a suit of clothes at a total cost of $1,134.74.

Tragedy struck the delegation when Chief Pushmataha died from pneumonia in Washington on Christmas Eve. Chief Apukshunnubbee had been killed en route to Washington as a result of a fall from a cliff. Chief Moshulatubbee, therefore, was the only district chief left in the delegation when the negotiations were concluded.

On January 20, 1825, Chief Moshulatubbee and Secretary of War John Calhoun signed the Treaty of 1825 (also called the Treaty of Washington City). The treaty redefined the eastern boundary of the Choctaw land in the newly designated Indian Territory (now Oklahoma) as a line extending from the Arkansas River near Fort Smith due south to the Red River, which is approximately the boundary between Arkansas and Oklahoma today. The Choctaw had ceded about 2 million acres of the land given to them at Doak's Stand, but in return the U.S. government agreed to move all white settlers living to the west of the new boundary out of the Choctaw's territory and not to permit any more whites to cross this border. In addition, the Choctaw received a perpetual annuity of $6,000, a waiver of back debts they owed to trading companies, and pensions for all Choctaw veterans who fought in the War of 1812.

The United States now hoped that the Choctaw would voluntarily remove to Indian Territory. A few did in the late 1820s, and by 1829 a small settlement, later known as Skullyville, was established near Fort Smith, Arkansas. But this gradual emigration was too slow to suit the white settlers in Mississippi. In 1829, the Mississippi state legislature extended its laws over the Choctaw, and in January 1830 the Choctaw were granted Mississippi citizenship, and their tribal government was abolished. When Choctaw leaders then began to challenge the pressures put on them by the U.S. and Mississippi governments, the United States decided that another treaty was needed to induce the Choctaw to remove to Indian Territory and to secure the more than 10 million acres of land the tribe still retained in Mississippi and Alabama.

Chief Moshulatubbee in an 1834 painting by George Catlin.

President Andrew Jackson sent Secretary of State John H. Eaton and Colonel John Coffee to negotiate the treaty in September 1830. Choctaw leaders Greenwood LeFlore, Moshulatubbee, and Nitakechi, with about 6,000 Choctaws, met them between the two prongs of Dancing Rabbit Creek in present-day Noxubee County in east Mississippi. The meeting officially opened on September 18 in a festive atmosphere. During the day, Eaton and Coffee made speeches, which John Pitchlynn, a white man who had long lived among the Choctaw, interpreted to the tribe. In the evening, many Choc-

After negotiating the Choctaw removal treaty, Greenwood LeFlore became so unpopular with the inhabitants of his district that they held a special election to depose him as chief.

taw danced and visited the saloons and gambling tables that had been set up inside tents on the treaty grounds. The U.S. officials did not permit missionaries and the converted Choctaw to camp on the grounds because they feared the Christian Indians would object to the consumption of alcohol and interfere with the negotiations.

Over the next few days, the Choctaw leaders discussed the details of the proposed treaty with Eaton and Coffee. During their meetings, as many as 60 councilmen would sit in a circle, with a small number of selected older Choctaw women seated in the center. Although the women did not participate actively in the discussions, they let their feelings be known to the councilmen before and after the meetings.

On Wednesday, September 22, the Choctaw voted on whether to accept the treaty. Only one Choctaw leader, Killihota, favored removal. When the next day the Choctaw voted against removal a second time, Secretary Eaton became irate. He threatened that if the Choctaw refused to sign the treaty the president would declare war against the tribe and send troops into their territory. By Friday, September 24, negotiations had broken down, and many Choctaw left the treaty grounds. Sensing that those who remained were inclined toward removal, Eaton and Coffee asked Greenwood LeFlore to help them draft another treaty. They knew LeFlore, the chief of the Upper Towns district (formerly known as Okla Falaya), was a removal supporter and that he had a strong following among the mixed-blood members of the tribe. Talks continued over the next several days about the specific provisions of the treaty while Eaton coerced and intimidated the Choctaw.

Finally, on Monday, September 27, 172 Choctaw leaders, led by LeFlore and Moshulatubbee, signed the Treaty of Dancing Rabbit Creek. In it, the Choctaw ceded their remaining land in Mississippi and agreed to move to Indian Territory. In return the United States promised to protect the Choctaw in their new homeland and guaranteed the tribe an annuity of $20,000 for 20 years and additional money to build schools, churches, and a council house there. However, the treaty's Article 14, a contribution of LeFlore, gave the Choctaw an opportunity to remain in Mississippi. It stated that a Choctaw family could elect to stay and become citizens of the United States as long as the family head registered this intention with the Choctaw agent in Mississippi within six months. The head of the family would then receive 640 acres of land, plus an additional 320 acres for each child over 10 years of age living with the family and 160 acres for each child under 10. With the signing of this treaty, the story of two separate groups of Choctaw—one in Indian Territory and one in Mississippi—would begin.

While the Choctaw chiefs and the U.S. government negotiated the treaties that ultimately resulted in the tribe's division and loss of its homeland, the daily life of the average Choctaw was undergoing tremendous social and cultural changes. The arrival of missionaries in 1818 produced perhaps the greatest of these. Like the U.S. government, missionaries attempted to "civilize" the Indians by teaching them the values of non-Indian society. Although the Choctaw, at least initially, did not embrace Christianity, they enthusiastically supported the schools that missionaries founded in their domain. For instance, Elliot, the first Choctaw school, was initially funded by the Presbyterian mission board, but the Choctaw soon offered the instructors the $200 annual interest payment they

received from the federal government as a result of the Treaty of Fort St. Stephens. The Choctaw people also donated $500 a year, and by 1820 the Choctaw council had agreed to pay $6,000 annually for 17 years to support the school. Shortly after Elliot was established in 1818, Methodist and Baptist missionaries came to practice among the Choctaw. By 1825, 13 mission schools were operating in Choctaw country.

In these schools, the missionaries taught many Choctaw children to read

This 600-year-old pipe bowl was used at the signing of the Treaty of Dancing Rabbit Creek in 1830.

and write in the Choctaw language with the Roman alphabet, the same alphabet used to write in English. They also trained them in innovations in agriculture, animal husbandry, and homemaking. During this time, the Choctaw began to grow cotton, which students were taught to spin and weave into clothing. As the tribe became more educated, its economy came to rely less on hunting and more on industry and agriculture.

The Choctaw adopted the new ways readily in part because of the increasing influence and number of tribespeople of mixed Indian and white heritage. Several so-called mixed-bloods had be-

David Folsom, one of several young men of mixed Indian and white ancestry who gained political power within the tribe prior to removal.

come leaders in the tribe in the 1820s. The sons of Indian women and white men who had settled in Choctaw country in the late 18th century, Greenwood LeFlore, Peter Pitchlynn, and David Folsom were particularly well regarded within the tribe.

As the tribe's contact with white settlers increased, certain traditional Choctaw customs began to change. Because missionaries condemned the practices of their medicine men, some Choctaw stopped consulting their traditional healers. The tribe's distinctive burial practices were abandoned as well. They ceased to place their dead on a scaffold and no longer employed a bone picker. The Choctaw now buried their corpses in a sitting position surrounded by the deceased's personal possessions. The family would go to the grave to weep and cry; at the end of the mourning period a ceremony and a feast were held.

The Choctaw's system of justice also underwent a transformation. Traditionally, if a Choctaw committed a crime, he would be punished by the victim's relatives. If the accused could not be found, a member of his family was substituted; however, most violators voluntarily submitted to punishment. But now, a Choctaw charged with an offense was subject instead to a trial by a jury of light horsemen, the mounted patrols the Choctaw established to dispense justice. A band of light horsemen would travel through each district, serving as sheriffs as well as judges. For minor offenses, a criminal was lashed;

Choctaw light horsemen, such as these photographed in the late 19th century, traveled on horseback through the tribal lands to enforce Choctaw laws and punish all violators.

for major offenses such as murder, he was shot.

Despite these adaptations, the Choctaw retained much of their traditional way of life. They were still primarily agriculturalists, growing corn, beans, squash, and other crops; they continued to fish, hunt, and gather fruits and nuts to supplement the food supply; and they performed the same dances and played the same games the tribe had enjoyed for centuries. For the 300 years following the Choctaw's first contact with Europeans, the tribe had struggled to learn how to coexist with the white man by adopting elements of his society while maintaining its traditional Indian customs. Removal now presented the Choctaw with the new challenge of reconstructing this hybrid culture in an unfamiliar area hundreds of miles from their homeland. ▲

Nanih Waiya, the Choctaw's first council building in Indian Territory, which was erected near the present-day city of Tuskahoma, Oklahoma, in 1837.

4

STRUGGLE
AND
PROSPERITY

As soon as the Treaty of Dancing Rabbit Creek was signed in 1830, some Choctaw migrated to Indian Territory, hoping to claim the best land there. The majority of the Choctaw, however, waited to be removed in three successive journeys that the U.S. government scheduled for 1831, 1832, and 1833. The Bureau of Indian Affairs (BIA), the government office formed by the War Department in 1824 to deal with the Indians, planned to relocate each year about one-third of the Choctaw population, which at the time numbered between 18,000 and 20,000.

Anticipating the difficulty of transporting entire eastern tribes to distant Indian Territory, the BIA had chosen to remove the Choctaw first because of the tribe's long history of cooperation with the U.S. government. Secretary of War John Eaton gave the responsibility for preparing the removal to Agent George S. Gaines, whom the Choctaw knew and trusted. Gaines was dedicated to making the ordeal as easy on the tribe as possible, but the enormous task of organizing this 550-mile trek through unsettled country proved to be extremely complicated. The plans became especially muddled after Lewis Cass, who replaced Eaton as secretary of war in April 1831, dismissed many of the officials Gaines had hired to help with the removal.

In late fall of 1831, the first group of Choctaw made their way to Memphis and Vicksburg, two cities on the Mississippi River that served as their departure points. Gaines had secured five steamboats—the *Walter Scott*, the *Brandywine*, the *Reindeer*, the *Talma*, and the *Cleopatra*—that transported the Choctaw up the Mississippi to various tributaries, namely, the Ouachita, Arkansas, and White rivers. Other steamboats took the Indians northwest up these rivers as far as the boats could travel without being grounded in shallow water. The Choctaw then walked to Indian Territory from such towns as Ecore À Fabre, Washington, Little Rock, and Rockroe. Upon arrival, many Choctaw registered at Fort Towson, Mountain Fork, Old Miller Court House, and Horse Prairie, near the Red River in the southeastern corner of their new land, whereas others went to the Choctaw Agency near the Arkansas River in the northeastern section.

For this first party of Choctaw, removal was a bitter experience. The southern Mississippi valley had one of the worst snowstorms in its history in the winter of 1831. Because the BIA had not purchased enough provisions and equipment for the journey, few of the Choctaw had blankets, shoes, or winter clothing and many died in the zero-degree weather. Heavy rains also washed out some roads and trails, which made

their travel slower. Able to cover only 15 miles a day, the Choctaw soon depleted their already inadequate food supply, and hundreds more starved to death.

Morale among the Choctaw remaining in Mississippi was low after they heard reports of the first removal. Nevertheless, about 6,000 to 7,000 agreed to emigrate in the second group, which departed in October 1832. Although the journey began well, icy winds and rain again slowed travel, and many in the party became infected with cholera, a disease that proved fatal in most cases. Because the cost of the first removal had been twice what the BIA had anticipated, Cass had fired Gaines and put the U.S. Army in charge of preparing the next two expeditions. To economize, the army had reduced the food rations for each Choctaw and ordered only five small wagons for every

The Cleopatra, *one of five steamboats used to transport Choctaw in the 1841 removal party up the Mississippi River.*

REMOVAL ROUTES OF THE CHOCTAW, 1831–1833

thousand Indians, so that even the elderly and infirm had to walk the last leg of their journey. William Armstrong, an army captain who assisted in the second removal, observed, "Fortunately, they are a people that will walk to the last, or I do not know how we could go on." News of these horrors discouraged most of the Choctaw still in Mississippi from joining the third removal party in December 1833. Although good weather made this journey much easier than the previous ones, there were only 900 Choctaw in this group. After they arrived in Indian Territory in the spring of 1834, the Choctaw population there was approximately 11,500. A total of about 14,000 Choctaw had left Mississippi in the 3 removal parties, but at least 2,500 had died during the travel west.

The tribespeople who remained in their homeland, however, did not fare much better than those who removed.

Secretary of War Lewis Cass, who was charged with being careless and inefficient in his efforts to organize the removal of eastern Indian tribes.

According to Article 14 of the Treaty of Dancing Rabbit Creek, every Choctaw family that elected to stay in Mississippi had to register with the Choctaw Agency within six months in order to be eligible for land ownership. But Colonel William Ward, the U.S. agent for the Mississippi Choctaw at the time, refused to let some of the Indians register. Ward lost or misplaced the records of many of those he did register, and in some cases he simply removed names from his lists. Ward was particularly hesitant to register full-bloods, because he hoped that they especially would choose to remove to Indian Territory. Although the Bureau of Indian Affairs did not condone Colonel Ward's actions, it did little to curtail them. While John Eaton was secretary of war, he had even dispatched a cavalry to Mississippi to see that the Choctaw, particularly the full-bloods, were encouraged to emigrate. Many Indians turned to the government of Mississippi for help and protection, but the state, which was busy selling the ceded Choctaw homeland to land speculators and settlers, offered little assistance. Although Colonel Ward was finally dismissed by the U.S. government in 1833, allegedly because there were not enough Indians left in Mississippi to justify an agent, only 69 heads of Choctaw families—30 full-bloods and 39 mixed-bloods—were ever officially registered. The vast majority of the approximately 6,000 Choctaw who remained in Mississippi, therefore, never received the land to which they were entitled.

Life for the Mississippi Choctaw was difficult throughout the 1830s. Many suffered from poverty and hunger, and their standard of living was described by observers at the time as lower than that of the black slaves in the state. Because most of the missionaries among the Choctaw had removed with the majority of the tribe, these Indians no longer had access to schools or churches. Whites continually harassed them, often fining or imprisoning them for minor infractions or burning their houses and tearing down their fences. Most of the Mississippi Choctaw became squatters, landless settlers who lived in isolated areas on poor farmland to which they had no legal title. To survive, they gathered wild berries and nuts and planted corn, pumpkins, and potatoes, and some raised chickens and hogs. A few worked on nearby farms of white settlers, earning 50 cents a day for picking and hoeing cotton. But despite their situation, these dispossessed Choctaw retained their tribal identity. They were still bonded by language and custom, even though they no longer had any common land or government.

Once the Choctaw in Indian Territory had recovered from the trauma of removal, their experience was much different from that of their Mississippi kin. In possession of a vast expanse of land and regular annuity income, they were able immediately to begin to rebuild the culture they had in Missis-

sippi. First they established settlements close to the eastern border of their territory in three districts, which they named after the chiefs who had negotiated the Treaty of Doak's Stand. Pushmataha, to the west of the Kiamichi River, was settled by Chief Nitakechi's followers; Apukshunnubbee, to the east of the Kiamichi, by Chief LeFlore's; and Moshulatubbee, north of the other two districts and south of the Arkansas and Canadian rivers, by Chief Moshulatubbee's. Moshulatubbee and Nitakechi led their people to these areas, but Greenwood LeFlore had decided to stay in Mississippi despite his earlier support for the tribe's removal. His nephew George W. Harkins and later his cousin Thomas LeFlore succeeded him as chief.

The Choctaw wasted no time in developing their new land. They soon began to farm along the floodplains of the Arkansas, Red, and Kiamichi rivers and to raise cattle, sheep, and horses in the hillier regions of their territory. In the fall of 1833, only months after the second removal, the Choctaw had already produced a surplus of 40,000 bushels of corn, which they sold to the U.S. government to aid future Choctaw immigrants. Within a few years, the Choctaw were also raising potatoes, peas, beans, oats, rye, wheat, pumpkins, and melons. Cotton as well was grown on large plantations along the Red River. These were farmed with the help of black slaves that a few Choctaw slave owners had brought from Mississippi.

The Choctaw soon established several small but prosperous towns along trails that were traveled by easterners migrating to Texas or to California. Among the earliest were Skullyville and Perryville in Moshulatubbee, Doaksville and Eagletown in Apukshunnubbee, and Boggy Depot in Pushmataha. Boggy Depot's location at the junction of two trails made it a major trading center, and Doaksville eventually became the largest town in Indian Territory.

George W. Harkins, chief of the Apukshunnubbee district. On the way to Indian Territory, Harkins told his followers that "ere long we shall reach our destined home, and . . . nothing short of the basest act of treachery will ever be able to wrest it from us."

The Choctaw held their first tribal council meeting in Indian Territory at Jack's Fork, at the center of the three districts, in 1834. There, on June 3, the tribe adopted a new constitution for the Choctaw Nation. Written in both Choctaw and English, it provided that all national business would be transacted by a general council composed of the 3 chiefs and 27 councilmen, 9 from each district. Only this general council would have the power to pass a law, which would have to be supported by two-thirds of the council members before it could be enacted. In 1837, the Choctaw erected a large log council house at Jack's Fork. They named the building Nanih Waiya after the sacred mound in the Choctaw's Mississippi homeland.

As quickly as possible, the tribal government set about forming a new Choctaw school system. The missionaries who had removed with the tribe established mission schools soon after they arrived in Indian Territory. The first, Wheelock Mission, was founded by Alfred Wright, a Presbyterian physician, in 1832. During the winter of 1833, the Choctaw began to open their own schools, funded by their annuities. By 1836, they had established 8 schools in addition to the 11 mission schools then operating in the Choctaw Nation. In 1843, the Choctaw council also began to provide financial support for boarding schools and Sunday schools. In the latter, adult Choctaw were instructed in elementary arithmetic and in reading and writing the Choctaw language.

Armstrong Academy, shown here in a 1910 photograph, was opened in 1843 and became one of the best institutions in the extensive Choctaw school system. During the late 19th century, this building served as the capitol of the Choctaw Nation and was renamed Chahta Tamaha, meaning Choctaw City.

In the early 1840s, Chief Nitakechi returned to Mississippi to encourage his kin to give up their meager existence there and emigrate to Indian Territory. After suffering from poverty, neglect, and continuous pressure to remove for more than a decade, most of the Mississippi Choctaw were anxious to join the thriving Choctaw Nation. Between 1845 and 1854, 5,720 Mississippi Choctaw migrated west, 4,523 during the first 3 years alone. A census taken by Agent Douglas H. Cooper in 1853 listed only 2,069 Choctaw in Mississippi and 193 more in Louisiana.

The population of the Choctaw Nation also increased during the 1840s and 1850s because many Chickasaw settled there. The Chickasaw had agreed in 1830 to cede their homeland in northern Mississippi and Alabama to the United States in exchange for land in Indian Territory, shrewdly negotiating for the right to choose this tract themselves. The Chickasaw sent several exploring parties to search for their new western

(continued on page 58)

A GAME OF ISHTABOLI

George Catlin was born at Wilkes-Barre, Pennsylvania, in 1796. He attended law school and practiced as an attorney before deciding to pursue his first love, painting. He quickly became a noted portraitist in Philadelphia and received commissions to paint a number of prominent people, among them President James Monroe, former president James Madison, and Madison's wife, Dolley. In the late 1820s, Catlin visited several nearby Indian reservations, where he painted members of the Seneca, Oneida, Ottawa, and Mohegan tribes.

Fascinated by these tribespeople and their ways of life, Catlin left Philadephia in 1830, journeying west in order to observe and paint other tribes and their villages. For six years Catlin journeyed up the Mississippi and Missouri rivers and over the plains of the Southwest, visiting some 48 tribes and capturing their daily lives in hundreds of paintings. These works combined with the journal Catlin kept during his travels constitute one of the most comprehensive eyewitness records of the Indians on the American frontier.

Catlin visited the Choctaw Nation in the summer of 1834. Impressed by the tribe's enthusiasm for their summertime entertainments, he wrote, "The most beautiful was decidedly the ball-playing . . . . have sat, and almost dropped from my horse's back with irresistible laughter at the succession of droll tricks and kicks and scuffles which ensue in the almost superhuman struggles for the ball." Catlin watched a game of ishtaboli near Skullyville, which he painted and described in his book Letters and Notes on the Manners, Customs, and Conditions of the North American Indians:

Monday afternoon, at three o'clock, I rode out to a pretty prairie, the ball-play-ground of the Choctaws. . . . There were two points of timber about half a mile apart, in which the two parties for the play, with their respective families and friends were encamped.

All preparations were made by some old men who were selected to be the judges. They drew a line from one goal to the other. Immediately from the woods on both sides of the field a great concourse of women and old men, boys and girls, dogs and horses came up to the line drawn across the center of the field to place their bets. The betting was all done across this line. It seemed to be chiefly left to the women who martialled out a little of everything their houses and their fields contained: Goods and chattels, knives, dresses, blankets, pots and kettles, dogs and horses and guns. All

Catlin's 1834 portrait of Tullock-chisk-ko (He who drinks the juice of the stone), the Choctaw's champion ballplayer. In addition to the traditional ballplay tail, loincloth, and belt, Tullock-chisk-ko wears a mane of horsehair.

were placed in the possession of stake-holders, who sat by them and watched them all night preparatory to the play.

This game had been arranged and "made up" three or four months before the parties met to play it, in the following manner: The two champions who led the two parties chose players alternately from the whole tribe. They each sent runners with ball-sticks, fantastically ornamented with ribbons and red paint, to be touched by each one of the chosen players, who thereby agreed to be on the spot at the appointed time and ready for the play.

Once the field was prepared, and preliminaries of the game all settled, the bettings all made and goods all "staked," night came on without the appearance of any players on the ground. But soon after dark, a procession of lighted flambeaux [torches] was seen coming from each encampment. The players assembled around their respective goals. At the beat of the drums and chants of the women, each party of players commenced the "ball-play dance." Each party danced for a quarter of an hour around their respective goals in their ball-play dress; rattling their ball-sticks together in the most violent manner, and all singing as loud as they could. Meanwhile, the women of each party, who had their goods at stake, formed into two rows on the line between the two parties of players, and also danced in a uniform step, all their voices joined in chants to the Great Spirit. In the meantime, four old medicine-men, who were to be the judges of the play, were seated at midfield. They were busily smoking to the Great Spirit, too, for their success in judging rightly between the parties in so important an affair.

The dance was repeated at intervals of every half hour all night. The players were certainly awake all night, but prepared for play the next morning.

In the morning, at the appointed hour, the game commenced with the judges throwing up the ball and firing a gun. An instant struggle ensued between the players, as some six or seven hundred men mutually endeavored to catch the ball in their sticks and throw it into their opponent's goal. Hundreds ran together and leapt over each other's heads, and darted between their adversaries legs, tripping and throwing and foiling each other in every possible manner. Every voice was raised in shrill yelps and barks. There were rapid successions of feats, and of incidents.

Every trick is used that can be devised, to oppose the progress of the ball. These obstructions often meet desperate resistance, which terminate in a violent scuffle, and sometimes fisticuffs. Sticks are dropped, and the parties are unmolested as they settle it between themselves.

"In these desperate struggles for the ball, hundreds of strong young Indian athletes were running together and leaping . . . foiling each other in every possible manner."

At times, when the ball is on the ground, such a confused mass rushes around it, and knocks their sticks together, there is no possibility of anyone seeing it. The condensed mass of ball-sticks, and shins, and bloody noses, travels around the different parts of the field for a quarter of an hour at a time. Since no one can see the ball, several minutes may pass while the mob struggles even though the ball is being played over another part of the field.

Each time the ball passes between the stakes of either party, one point is counted for game, and there is a halt of about one minute. Then play is started again by the judges. The struggle continues until the successful party gets to one hundred, which is the limit of the game. It was not finished until an hour before sunset. The winners take their stakes. Then, by previous agreement, a number of jugs of whisky were produced, which sent them all off merry and in good humor.

(continued from page 53)

home, but to the exasperation of the U.S. government, they stalled their removal by continually claiming they could not find any suitable land. In 1833, the Choctaw invited the Chickasaw to settle in their nation in an uninhabited area to the west of the Choctaw's own settlements, but the Chickasaw declined because they did not want to live on lands they did not own. Increasing pressure to remove, however, finally forced them to reconsider. In 1837, they signed the Treaty of Doaksville with the Choctaw, by which the Chickasaw agreed to pay $530,000 for the right to settle in the Choctaw Nation. The next year, the Choctaw council adopted a new constitution that created a fourth district for the Chickasaw immigrants. It also provided for the Chickasaw to elect one chief and nine councilmen to represent them.

Neither the Chickasaw nor the Choctaw were ever comfortable with this arrangement, however. The Chickasaw had little influence in the Choctaw government, because the Choctaw outnumbered them in council by three to one. The Choctaw never adjusted to sharing their nation and continued to regard the Chickasaw as intruders in their tribal affairs. Finally, both tribes agreed that the Chickasaw should have their own government. In the Treaty of 1855, which the United States also signed, the Chickasaw were given the right to establish their own council to govern the fourth district, which then

became the Chickasaw Nation. The Chickasaw's finances would be kept separate from the Choctaw's, but the tribes would hold in common the title to their lands. Citizens of each nation would also have citizenship in the other. In the treaty, the Choctaw agreed as well to lease all their land west of the new Chickasaw Nation to the United States for $800,000, half of which would be paid to the Chickasaw. The United States, according to this agreement, was to make this area the permanent home of the Wichita and several other tribes.

The Treaty of 1855 also settled an outstanding dispute between the U.S. government and the Choctaw. The 1830 Treaty of Dancing Rabbit Creek had stated that the Choctaw were entitled to all money received from the sale of their lands in Mississippi, minus the cost of their removal. Although removal expenses totaled approximately $5 million and their Mississippi lands were sold for about $8 million, the United States had not given the profit to the tribe. The Choctaw sent a delegation to Washington in 1853 to claim the money, but when they still received no response from the government, the tribe agreed in the 1855 treaty to allow the U.S. Senate to decide their case. In 1859, the Senate awarded the tribe $2,981,247.30, a substantial victory even though most of it eventually went to paying the Choctaw's legal fees.

In the winter of that year, a delegation of Choctaw traveled to North

Fork Village in the Creek Nation to meet in council with representatives of the Creek, Cherokee, Seminole, and Chickasaw. At this conference, these Indian tribes adopted a code of laws that would apply to all their people. They also agreed that a citizen of one of their nations could transfer his or her citizenship to another with the approval of the tribal governments involved. The Indian groups that joined this confederation later became known as the "five civilized tribes" because all had adopted many of the values of white culture.

Although the Choctaw had little contact with eastern settlers during their first three decades in Indian Territory, their political and social structure came more and more to resemble that of Americans of the period. By 1860, they had created the office of principal chief and a supreme court and had divided their general council into a sen-

Choctaw Indians in Louisiana, painted by the French artist Alfred Boisseau in 1847.

THE CHOCTAW NATION, 1855

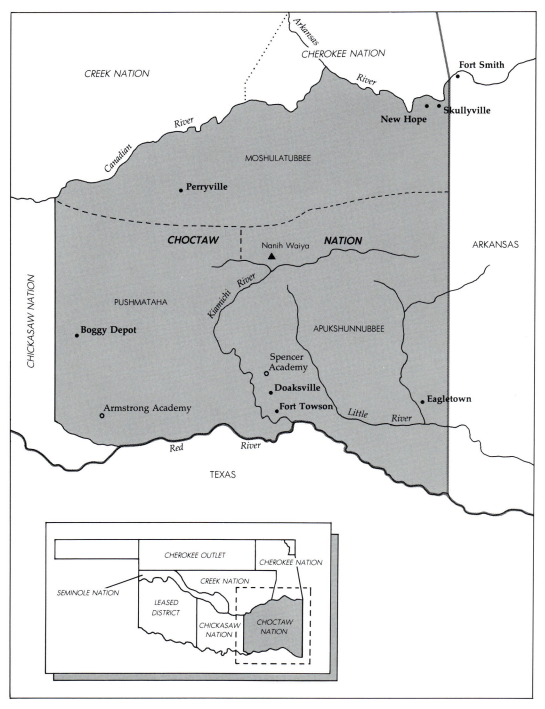

CREEK NATION

Arkansas

CHEROKEE NATION

Fort Smith

River

New Hope

Skullyville

Canadian   River

MOSHULATUBBEE

Perryville

CHOCTAW   NATION

Nanih Waiya

ARKANSAS

CHICKASAW NATION

Kiamichi River

PUSHMATAHA

APUKSHUNNUBBEE

Boggy Depot

Spencer
Academy

Doaksville

Eagletown

Armstrong Academy

Fort Towson

Little   River

Red   River

TEXAS

CHEROKEE OUTLET

CHEROKEE NATION

CREEK NATION

SEMINOLE NATION

LEASED
DISTRICT

CHICKASAW
NATION

CHOCTAW
NATION

ate and a house of representatives in conscious imitation of the U.S. government's executive, judicial, and legislative branches. The tribe's schools at the time enrolled approximately 900 students, who were taught in English using a curriculum similar to that of American schools of the day. Many Choctaw also had become Christians. Nearly one-fourth of the tribespeople belonged to the Presbyterian, Methodist, or Baptist churches by the beginning of the 1860s. Despite these changes from their traditional way of life, however, the Choctaw retained their independence. Left to their own devices, they had tamed a wild and remote frontier in an amazingly short amount of time. But this period of peace and prosperity for the Choctaw would soon end, however, as the United States once again pulled the tribe into its own conflicts at the onset of the American Civil War. ▲

*Principal Chief Green McCurtain and 1896 Choctaw councilmen
Victor M. Locke, Peter J. Hudson, and Dr. E. N. Wright (clockwise
from left).*

THE
END
OF A
NATION

When the American Civil War broke out in April 1861, tribal leaders hoped they would be able to keep the Choctaw Nation out of their conflict. The Choctaw chiefs immediately declared their neutrality to the commissioner of Indian affairs, but by June the tribe had already begun to reconsider its position. Douglas H. Cooper, who had been the Choctaw's agent for eight years and was well regarded by them, was an ardent advocate for the South. His influence helped to increase the Choctaw's growing support for the Confederacy. As slave owners, the Choctaw tended to sympathize with the South, and these leanings were intensified by their disappointment with the U.S. government.

At the beginning of the war, the United States had removed all of its armies from Indian Territory because this large area would require too many of its soldiers to defend against enemy attack. Without the military protection that the United States had guaranteed them in treaty after treaty, the Choctaw were not only vulnerable to Southern troops, but also to hostile settlers in Arkansas and Texas. The departure of Union forces left the tribe little choice but to ally itself with the Confederacy. On July 12, the Choctaw sent some members of their council to North Fork Village in the Creek Nation to meet with representatives of the Confederate government. There the Choctaw signed a treaty of allegiance in which the Confederacy promised to protect the Choctaw Nation and respect its independence.

Despite this alliance, few Choctaw fought in the Confederate army. Union forces destroyed the Confederate stores

Choctaw Agent Douglas H. Cooper, who influenced the tribe to ally itself with the Confederacy in 1861. During the Civil War, Cooper served as a general in the Confederate army.

in Perryville and captured the outpost at Skullyville in 1863, but otherwise their lands were not invaded. The Creek and the Cherokee nations, however, were occupied by Union troops for the last two years of the war. Confederate troops and refugees from these tribes escaped to Choctaw country, where the needs of the extra population caused a food shortage for the war's duration. The Choctaw were further impoverished by the loss of their annuity income. The United States had stopped paying annuities to the Choctaw when they allied themselves with the Confederacy, and the Confederate government had not provided for their payment as it had promised to do.

Following the defeat of the South, Chief Peter Pitchlynn surrendered the Choctaw's military forces to the U.S. government on June 19, 1865. In September, he led a Choctaw delegation to Fort Smith, Arkansas, where the commissioner of Indian affairs had called a council of all Confederate-allied Indian tribes. Although the delegation was anxious for the Choctaw Nation to resume relations with the United States, it resisted the terms of the peace treaty drafted by the government. In exchange for the protection of the U.S. Army and restoration of the tribal annuities, the Choctaw were to abolish slavery, to allow their freed black slaves to remain in their lands, and to surrender one-third of their territory, which the government planned to give to Kansas Indians who had supported the Union.

Although the Choctaw accepted a preliminary treaty with these provisions, the council instructed the delegation it sent to Washington to draw up the final treaty not to cede any territory occupied by Choctaw. Owing largely to the diplomatic skills of Peter Pitchlynn, the delegation succeeded in not surrendering any such territory. It did agree, however, to give up control of the Choctaw lands west of the Chickasaw Nation, which the U.S. government had been leasing since 1855. The United States planned to remove the Choctaw's black population to this area because the tribespeople objected to their slaves becoming citizens of the Choctaw Nation and thus becoming eligible

(continued on page 73)

TREASURES THAT PRESERVE TRADITION

The Choctaw who were forced to move to Indian Territory in the 1830s had to abandon much of their traditional culture. But memories of their Mississippi past remained, as objects crafted by generations of Choctaw in their new home attest. By embellishing functional objects that they made there using early methods, Indian Territory artisans in the 19th century created decorative treasures to remind them of their former homeland. Crafts also became a way for the western Choctaw to preserve some traditions that were quickly passing. Their dolls, for example, display the elegance and rich variety of Choctaw dress. By 1880, however, when they were sewn, such costumes were seldom worn as the Indians in the Choctaw Nation increasingly adopted the clothing styles of non-Indian Americans.

The Choctaw artists who remained in Mississippi in the 19th century were more able to resist acculturation, and they continued to use the same techniques and materials as the tribe had for centuries. Today Choctaw artisans in the Southeast still create beautiful baskets by dying and braiding strips of cane just as their ancestors did.

Baldric (shoulder strap) decorated with beadwork. Choctaw tribal leader Israel Folsom was given this baldric by his grandmother before he left for Indian Territory in 1832.

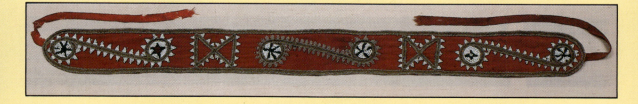

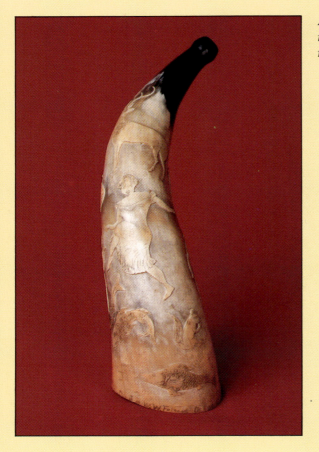

A gunpowder horn owned by the Folsom family that was decorated with carvings of animals and human figures in the 1860s.

Two spoons that were made from cow horns in the early 20th century.

A gunpowder horn with a leather hunting bag and gunpowder measure from the 1830s.

A 16-inch doll of a Mississippi Choctaw woman, sewn in 1933. Its body is cloth stuffed with sawdust, and its features are embroidered.

This Choctaw warrior doll from 1880 stands 22 inches tall and wears a blanket around its waist in the style of Plains Indians. The red dots on its cheeks and forehead represent face painting.

A 21-inch-tall doll of a male Choctaw from 1880 dressed in traditional buckskin leggings and moccasins. Dancers in Choctaw ceremonies today wear beaded shoulder straps much like these.

Basket made in Bayou Teche, Louisiana, in 1884. It has a 10-inch-square base and was used for carrying fruits and vegetables.

Also made in Louisiana in 1884, these small baskets, only 7 and 5 inches high, were probably intended as gifts.

Detail showing the finishing of the rim on Farve's basket.

Detail showing the multicolored twill pattern of Farve's basket.

This woven-cane basket, approximately 7 inches high and 5 inches in diameter, was made by Linda Farve of Pearl River, Mississippi, in 1984. Farve left some cane strips natural and used traditional dyes to color others red or black before she began to weave.

Strips of cane dyed brown and green create a geometric design against the natural cane on this basket, which was made in Mississippi.

A burden basket used for hauling gathered plants. The Mississippi Choctaw carried such baskets by placing the strap across their forehead and supporting the basket on their back.

(continued from page 64)

for a share of their tribal annuities. The U.S. government tried to induce the Choctaw to incorporate the freedmen into their Nation by offering the tribe $150,000 for the leased district on the condition that they allow the blacks to settle among them. Although the tribal government was deeply in debt, the council declined the money and asked the commissioner of Indian affairs to proceed with the removal of the freedmen. When the U.S. government was not able to have its way through negotiation, it tried another tack: The United States simply ignored the request and paid the Choctaw the $150,000, anyway.

The Choctaw themselves wanted to disregard several other provisions in the treaty. One stipulated that the Choctaw were to attend an annual council of all the tribes in Indian Territory. The U.S. government hoped that it could eventually abolish individual tribal governments and establish this council as the central government over the entire territory, a plan the Choctaw feared and resented because it threatened their Nation's independence. The Choctaw also resisted the treaty's specifications for a survey of their lands, which would be used to divide their territory if in the future they elected to give up common ownership of the tribal lands. The United States wanted to encourage the Choctaw to section off their territory into individually owned tracts, or allotments, but the tribespeople distrusted the program, as they remembered how few of their Mississippi kin

had received the land promised them by the U.S. government in 1830.

The provision of the Treaty of 1866 that had the greatest immediate effect on the tribe was its granting of permission for construction of a railroad across the Choctaw Nation. Even before the treaty was ratified, employees of Kansas railroad companies were racing to the border of Indian Territory. The first to get there was the Missouri, Kansas, and Texas Railroad, which was nicknamed "the Katy." Between the summer of 1870 and the spring of 1872, it built a line running north to south through the Cherokee, Creek, and Choctaw Nations. The Choctaw council became angry because the Katy had paid them nothing for the use of their land. Its complaints received little attention, however, especially after 1871 when Congress passed a law stating that railroad companies needed only congressional approval to construct lines through Indian Territory. Many more railroad lines were quickly built, including three additional ones through the Choctaw Nation during the next 20 years.

The coming of the railroads produced some dramatic changes in the Choctaw's way of life. Settlement patterns, for instance, were altered as many new towns sprang up along the rights of way. Older Choctaw towns and villages that were not near the railroads were virtually abandoned. The railroads also transformed the economy of the Choctaw Nation. Before the Civil War, some coal had been mined in the

(continued on page 77)

PETER PITCHLYNN
1806–1881

Peter Perkins Pitchlynn was born in 1806 to a part-Choctaw mother and an English father. Peter's grandfather, Isaac Pitchlynn, had traveled to Choctaw country in 1774, accompanied by his son John, to trade with the Indians. When Isaac died, John Pitchlynn decided to stay among the Choctaw and married Sophia Folsom. She was the daughter of a Choctaw woman and Nathaniel Folsom, one of three English brothers who had also settled in a Choctaw village in the 1770s.

Although Peter was only one-quarter Indian, his early life in some ways was similar to that of any Choctaw boy. Named Ha-tchoc-tuck-nee (Snapping Turtle) by his full-blood friends, he spent much of his youth hunting and playing Choctaw games. But as John Pitchlynn's son, Peter had much more exposure to the culture of white Americans than did his Choctaw contemporaries. The Pitchlynn trading post was visited by many eastern travelers who came through Choctaw country, and the family often entertained the white traders and missionaries who lived in the area. John Pitchlynn's position as English interpreter for the Choctaw also brought young Peter in contact with U.S. government officials.

This upbringing proved to be an ideal preparation for Peter Pitchlynn's career in politics and public service. During the 1820s, the Choctaw began to rely on young men of mixed white and Indian parentage such as Pitchlynn to negotiate treaties for them with the United States. More than most other tribespeople, these men possessed the knowledge of both English and the customs of white American society that were necessary to deal effectively with the federal officials. Elected to the tribal council in 1826 when he was only 20, Pitchlynn played an important role in drafting the first written Choctaw constitution. He made an even greater contribution to helping to negotiate the 1830 Treaty of Dancing Rabbit Creek in which the tribe ceded its homeland in exchange for land to the west in Indian Territory. Although he vigorously opposed removal, once it appeared inevitable, Pitchlynn shrewdly persuaded Secretary of War John Eaton to make several concessions in the treaty to the benefit of the Choctaw.

After the treaty was signed, Pitchlynn's popularity faded. The full-bloods in the tribe, most of whom did not want to remove to Indian Territory, felt betrayed by their mixed-blood leaders and accused the treaty negotiators of taking bribes from the federal government. To regain some of his lost favor, Peter accepted a post as superintendent of the Choctaw Academy in Kentucky in 1841. For several years the Choctaw, especially the full-bloods, had hoped that the federal government would close this eastern boarding school because they believed their children were learning little there other than the vices of white society, particularly drinking and gambling. Using the influence of his position, Pitchlynn convinced officials in Washington that the institution he headed was of no worth to the tribe. The federal government finally agreed to shut down the school and use the annuity funds that had

One of the few portraits of Pitchlynn that depict him wearing Indian dress is this 1834 painting by American artist George Catlin.

supported the Academy for schools located within the Choctaw Nation. The Choctaw rewarded Pitchlynn by electing him to the tribal council in 1842.

Pitchlynn's success in dealing with U.S. officials inspired him to spend more time in Washington. Throughout the late 1840s and the 1850s, he traveled to the capital to make claims on behalf of the Choctaw in Mississippi who had not received tracts of land that were promised to them in the Treaty of Dancing Rabbit Creek. In many cases, Pitchlynn won cash settlements for the claimants he represented, although he always deducted a substantial fee from the money collected.

Impressed by his skills as a claims representative, the tribe in 1853 selected Pitchlynn to be part of a delegation to present its own claim that the U.S. government owed the Choctaw the $3 million profit from the sale of their Mississippi lands. After pleading its case in Washington for six years, the delegation triumphed when the Senate agreed in 1859 that the money belonged to the tribe. It was also a personal triumph for Pitchlynn, for he had been guaranteed 10 percent of any award as his commission.

Pitchlynn at the age of 32. In 1842, the year Charles Fenderich painted this portrait, Pitchlynn had a chance meeting with the British novelist Charles Dickens aboard a steamboat. Dickens remembered him as "a remarkably handsome man . . . as stately and complete a gentleman of Nature's making as ever I beheld."

In 1861, when the outbreak of the Civil War seemed imminent, Pitchlynn returned to Indian Territory. He urged the Choctaw to remain loyal to the Union government, possibly because it had not yet paid in full either the 1859 award to the tribe or his commission. Pitchlynn failed to convince the Choctaw, however, and the tribe instead supported the Confederate states, a position Pitchlynn also came to adopt before the war had ended. The Choctaw, however, continued to perceive him as a Yankee sympathizer, which ironically worked to his political advantage. Anticipating the fall of the Confederacy and seeking a spokesperson who would have influence with the federal government, the tribespeople elected Pitchlynn as their chief in 1864. Their confidence in Pitchlynn was well placed. The Treaty of 1866 established peace between the Choctaw and the United States and required surprisingly few concessions from the tribe.

Pitchlynn's tenure as chief was brief. After he lost the election in 1866, he returned to Washington and devoted the rest of his life to attempting to secure the funds that the U.S. government owed to the tribe according to the 1859 Senate ruling and the 1866 treaty. Pitchlynn did not live to see the outcome of his efforts, however, as the U.S. government did not pay the money it owed the Choctaw until after his death in 1881. Pitchlynn was buried in the Congressional Cemetery in Washington, a non-Indian burial ground. This was appropriate, for he had lived most of his adult life in white American society. But it is equally appropriate that Pitchlynn's grave is near to that of the great Choctaw chief Pushmataha, who had died in Washington while negotiating the Treaty of 1825. Like Pushmataha, Pitchlynn spent his last days far from his homeland in the service of his people.

(continued from page 73)

area, but only for use by local black-smiths. The railroads, however, made it easy to transport coal to the East, where there was a strong demand for the mineral to fuel the growing steel industry.

Mine operators soon flocked to the mineral-rich lands of the Choctaw. One of the first of these was J. J. McAlester, a white store owner from Fort Smith, Arkansas. The Choctaw constitution granted that any citizen who discovered minerals in the Choctaw Nation was en-titled to own and operate a mine there. McAlester, who had married a Chick-asaw woman and therefore had Choc-taw citizenship, formed a company to develop mines in the tribal territory, which he then leased to mine operators for a royalty, or percentage of their prof-its. When McAlester refused to hand his royalties over to the Choctaw Nation and cited the provision in the consti-tution, Chief Coleman Cole was out-raged and, contrary to the laws of the Nation, ordered McAlester's execution. McAlester escaped, and thereafter half of the income of all mine owners in Choctaw country was paid to the tribal government.

With the rapid growth of the mining industry, the composition of the pop-

Coal loaded onto cars of the Missouri, Kansas, and Texas Railroad in the late 1870s near the town of McAlester in the Moshulatubbee district.

ulation of the Choctaw Nation changed radically. Mines were operated primarily by white men who recently arrived from Europe, including Czechs, Slovaks, Hungarians, Belgians, Germans, French, English, Swedes, and Italians. As mining increased, American miners from eastern coalfields and blacks from Texas also immigrated to Indian Territory. The developing lumber industry, made possible by the railroads, attracted additional white workers to Choctaw lands. In 1885, a census of the Choctaw Nation counted 12,816 Indians, 427 whites, and 38 blacks. In 1890, a survey listed 10,017 Indians, 28,345 whites, and 4,406 blacks. Although the tribal income increased greatly because of the new industries, the Choctaw had quickly become outnumbered in their own country.

Despite the overwhelming numbers of intruders, the Choctaw resisted social contact with both whites and blacks. They preferred to practice many of their traditional customs, and most

A Choctaw-operated sawmill in 1901. Mills such as this one supplied the growing population of the Choctaw Nation with wooden telegraph poles, fence posts, railroad ties, bridge timber, and lumber for the construction of buildings.

continued to farm, hunt, and fish for their livelihood. The American customs that most influenced the western Choctaw in the last decades of the 19th century were those that had been introduced to them by missionaries before their removal, namely, Christianity and education. Although missionaries had fallen out of favor somewhat with the tribe, their religion had not. The Baptist faith in particular was practiced by a large number of the Choctaw in Indian Territory.

One of the converted, Peter Folsom, traveled to Mississippi to establish a Baptist church for his fellow tribespeople there in 1879. Many other missionaries came to work among the Mississippi Choctaw during this period. After the Civil War, the lot of these Indians had improved as more became tenant farmers, who rented the fields they worked from landowners, instead of squatters. Yet the Choctaw in Mississippi were still a poor people, and therefore they welcomed the religion and services the missionaries offered them. In Mississippi, there were 8 Baptist ministers and 9 Baptist churches, which served approximately 300 Choctaw, by 1891. Methodist and Catholic churches as well as several mission schools were established for these Indians in the late 1890s.

During the Civil War, the Choctaw in Indian Territory had been forced to close their schools because of the lack of tribal funds, but as soon as the annuities were restored, the tribal government began to revive its educational

system. It first reopened two of the Nation's finest boarding schools, Spencer Academy for boys and New Hope Seminary for girls. As national revenues grew, other boarding schools and neighborhood schools resumed operation, and the council began to send the Choctaw's most promising students to the best American universities. At the end of the 19th century, the Choctaw Nation had a much better educated population than any of the states that bordered it. There were also many more literate Indians than whites within the Nation, for as noncitizens whites were not permitted to attend the tribe's public schools.

Without citizenship, the white inhabitants of the Choctaw Nation were denied other important privileges. Although they paid taxes to the Choctaw council, they had no representation in it. Nor could whites own the land on which they built their homes and businesses because the territory of the Nation was still tribally owned. As they became the majority of the population, the white settlers resented more and more having no rights to property and no political power, and they repeatedly appealed to the U.S. government to dissolve the Choctaw government and the tribal ownership of its land. This pressure increased after 1889, when the United States organized Oklahoma Territory from the western portion of Indian Territory and opened this area to white settlement. Indian Territory was then reduced to only the lands of the Five Civilized Tribes and of the Indian

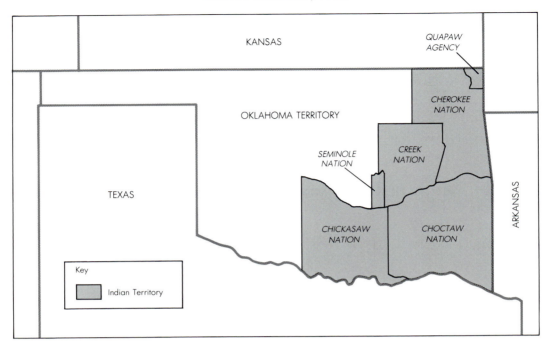

groups who lived in the northeastern corner of the territory under the jurisdiction of the Quapaw Agency.

On March 3, 1893, Congress passed a bill that gave President Grover Cleveland the right to form a committee of commissioners to negotiate the termination of the Five Civilized Tribes' land titles either by persuading the Indians to allot their territory to individuals or to cede it to the United States. The resulting committee, known as the Dawes Commission after committee chairman Henry L. Dawes, first approached the Choctaw in February 1894 with a proposal for the allotment of land in the Choctaw Nation. The tribe rejected the plan, but when the commission persisted, the Choctaw organized a com-

mittee of three tribespeople who spoke both English and Choctaw to escort the U.S. commissioners throughout the nation. The tribe hoped that once the Dawes Commission witnessed the Choctaw's progress and heard firsthand the people's resistance to allotment, it would leave the tribe alone. The commissioners, however, did not appear to appreciate the tribe's attachment to its institutions and merely pressed the Choctaw leaders harder to negotiate.

As it became obvious that the Dawes Commission would not give up, some Choctaw began to favor allotment. They feared that the U.S. government might take their land by force if the tribe did not cooperate. The leader of this faction was Green McCurtain, who was elected principal chief in the fall of 1895. Although most Choctaw still opposed allotment, this majority split its votes among three other candidates, who all supported preserving tribal ownership of their lands.

Against the wishes of the majority of the Choctaw, McCurtain formed a committee of nine council members, including himself, to negotiate with the Dawes Commission soon after the election. The committee met with the commissioners in December at the town of Muskogee in the Cherokee Nation and there agreed to give the United States title to the Choctaw's and Chickasaw's territory. The United States was to divide this land equally among all the citizens of these Indian Nations, except for the black freedmen, who would receive only 40 acres. The land occupied by towns and public buildings would be sold, and all citizens, excluding blacks, would be given a share of the proceeds. Mines within the Nations' territory would also be sold, but the U.S. government was to use the money for schools in the area. The tribal government would stay in place until March 1905 to oversee the allotment process.

The Choctaw committee signed an agreement at Muskogee on December 18, but the Chickasaw council rejected the plan, and Congress refused to ratify the agreement without the Chickasaw's approval. In April, McCurtain and his committee met with Chickasaw representatives in Atoka in the Pushmataha

district to try to convince them of the wisdom of allotment. McCurtain succeeded and with the United States the two tribes drafted the Atoka Agreement. Aside from a few administrative details, this called for the same allotment program as described in the Muskogee document.

As soon as the Atoka Agreement was signed, the Dawes Commission set about compiling a roll that would list everyone entitled to an allotment. This process was complicated when many

Hundreds of Mississippi Choctaw traveled to the Choctaw Nation by train in order to claim an allotment in Indian Territory. Many became the prey of greedy land speculators, who illegally bought these Choctaws' allotments for far less than the land's value.

The senate of the last council of the Choctaw Nation in 1905.

people who claimed to be Choctaw, but who had never lived in and were not citizens of the Choctaw Nation, applied for an allotment. In 1900, Congress legislated that these applications were not valid, although it did make an exception for Choctaw in Mississippi. The law stated that Mississippi Choctaw were entitled to an allotment if they agreed to live on the land granted them and if they could prove that they were descendants of the Choctaw who had requested tracts in their homeland in 1830 according to the terms of the Treaty of Dancing Rabbit Creek. Colonel William Ward, the agent who had the responsibility of registering these requests, had left very poor records, however. Unable to verify the claimants' descent, the U.S. government was flooded with more than 6,000 applications for allotment, most of which were fraudulent. Many of the actual descendants refused to come forward because they were afraid that the promise of tracts of land in Indian Territory was just another scheme of the U.S. government to steal their Mississippi homes. At least 300 did travel west by train to claim their allotments in 1903, and others were later brought to Indian Territory by land speculators who were eager to cheat the Indians out of the land they would receive.

The freedmen in the Choctaw Nation further complicated the work of the Dawes Commission by objecting to the 40-acre limit placed on their allotments by the Atoka Agreement. Many claimed that they had one Choctaw parent or grandparent and therefore were eligible for as large a tract of land as other mixed-blood Choctaw citizens. Although the Senate sent a committee to investigate these claims in 1906, the U.S. government closed the tribal rolls on March 4, 1907, with many disputes outstanding. The final roll listed 18,981 Indian citizens of the Choctaw Nation, 1,639 Mississippi Choctaw, and 5,994 former black slaves.

Throughout the long allotment process, the white settlers in the Choctaw Nation had been eager for the creation of a local government in which they would be represented. The Atoka Agreement had provided that the Choctaw government would stay in place until March 1905, but because the roll had taken much longer to compile than expected, this date was extended to April 1906. After all tribal governments were dissolved, the United States planned to merge Indian Territory and the newly formed Oklahoma Territory into a state. The Choctaw made one last attempt to maintain some control over their lands by sending delegates to a conference of representatives of the Five Civilized Tribes in Muskogee in July 1905. There the Indians drew up a constitution for a separate state that would be formed from Indian Territory only. The tribes decided to name their state Sequoyah in honor of the Cherokee leader who invented his tribe's written language.

The Congress refused to acknowledge the document, however, and on November 16, 1907, eight months after the tribal roll was compiled, the Choctaw became citizens of the state of Oklahoma. Despite decades of the tribe's constant effort to preserve its independence, the Choctaw Nation had come to an end. ▲

Women of the Mississippi Band of the Choctaw weaving swamp cane into baskets.

A
DIVIDED PEOPLE
CONTINUES

In the 1830s, the U.S. government had removed Indians to territory in the West to accommodate white settlers on the homelands of eastern tribes. In the 1880s, when settlers hungered for the Indians' new territory, the government proposed dividing Indian land into individually owned allotments as its new solution. The United States hoped that allotment would free this territory for white settlement as well as encourage Indians to become farmers and assimilate into the non-Indian mainstream society. This would at last relieve the federal government of having to deal with a large population within its borders who did not share the culture of the majority of Americans.

After the Choctaw received their allotments, many quickly sold their land, often for less than its actual value, to greedy white land speculators. The government attempted to discourage such sales but was not extremely successful, and most Choctaw lost their original allotment of land. The tribes-people soon scattered across Oklahoma, and as the government wished, they lost their tribal unity as a result.

The Choctaw in Oklahoma adopted many American customs and habits, but most continued to farm, especially cotton and corn, until much of the best farmland in the former Choctaw Nation had been sold to non-Indians. With their traditional means of earning a living gone, many of the Oklahoma Choctaw began to take jobs in the timber and mining industries and later in manufacturing.

Although their tribal government had been dissolved in 1906, the federal government still allowed the Choctaw in Oklahoma to have a principal chief to conduct certain continuing tribal affairs. Instead of being elected, however, the principal chiefs, following allotment, were appointed by the president of the United States and served under the supervision of the Bureau of Indian

Affairs. One of the major tasks that faced the first several appointed principal chiefs became pressing the U.S. government to sell the tribe's public land and to distribute the income to the Choctaw people as the Atoka Agreement specified. By 1920, all enrolled Choctaw or their heirs at last had received approximately $1,070 each from land sales. However, the government did not make payments on the sale of their mineral reserves until 1949.

When the Dawes Commission had closed its tribal roll book in 1907, more than 1,000 Choctaw remained in Mississippi. Unlike their Oklahoma kin, the Mississippi Choctaw were able to retain their group identity and many of their traditional customs, yet most continued to live in poverty. After nearly 80 years of ignoring the suffering of this branch of the tribe, Congress investigated the living conditions of the Choctaw in Mississippi in 1908 and 1916. The findings

A Mississippi Choctaw family on the porch of their home. This photograph was taken in 1908 by Mark R. Harrington, who was hired by collector George Heye to visit various tribes and purchase artifacts from them. The traditional mortar and pestle, which the woman at the right is using to remove kernels from corncobs, was one of Harrington's purchases. It now belongs to the Museum of the American Indian, which was founded by Heye.

Key

☐ Choctaw community with population of 500 or more

☐ Choctaw community with population of less than 500

○ County seat

convinced Secretary of the Interior Franklin Lane, who was now overseeing the Bureau of Indian Affairs, and President Woodrow Wilson that these Choctaw needed help. In 1918, the BIA established the Choctaw Indian Agency in Philadelphia, Mississippi, to direct various programs aimed at improving the general welfare of the members of the tribe in this state. Initially the government authorized a budget of $75,000, which the agency allocated in equal parts for farmland, farm supplies, and education. In 1920, the agency started a program for the establishment of day schools, and within 15 years

Harry J. W. Belvin, principal chief of the Oklahoma Choctaw from 1948 to 1975.

there was an elementary school in each of the Mississippi Choctaw's seven settlements: Pearl River, Conehatta, Bogue Chitto, Redwater, Tucker, Standing Pine, and Bogue Homa. The agency also launched a land-purchase program in 1921 through which the federal government, on behalf of the Choctaw, bought land in Neshoba County, in which most of the Choctaw lived, and in three neighboring counties settled by the tribe.

The aid provided to the Mississippi Choctaw reflects the changing policy of the U.S. government toward the American Indian in the 1920s. In 1926, the secretary of the interior commissioned a study of the Bureau of Indian Affairs. It concluded that the United States had

not acted responsibly when it dissolved tribal governments and allotted Indian land without providing these tribespeople with the education or job training to develop economically. In 1934, Congress put the proposals made in this report into action by passing the Indian Reorganization Act (Wheeler-Howard Act), which prohibited further allotment of land and permitted the organization of new tribal governments. As a result, the Oklahoma Choctaw formed a delegation consisting of 1 representative from each of the 10 counties in the area that had once been the Choctaw Nation. This delegation met at the Goodland Indian School near Hugo, Oklahoma, in 1934 and established an Advisory Council, the first council these Indians had since their government was dissolved in 1906. In 1948, the western branch of the Choctaw began again to elect its principal chiefs. That year, the tribespeople chose Harry J. W. Belvin as their chief, a position he would hold for the next 27 years.

In 1944, the secretary of the interior announced that the more than 16,000 acres of land that the federal government had purchased for the Mississippi Choctaw would become a reservation. In the following year, the secretary sanctioned the adoption of a constitution and bylaws that officially established the Mississippi Band of Choctaw Indians. The Mississippi Choctaw were now formally recognized by the United States and able to organize their own tribal government. They established an office of tribal chairman, who would be appointed by a council comprising of 16 members, elected from the 7 communities, with the number from each in proportion to its population.

In August 1953, the U.S. government reversed its policy toward the American Indian when Congress passed House Concurrent Resolution 108, which became known as the Termination Act. The intent of the resolution was to terminate, or bring to an end, the federal government's involvement with Indian tribes on reservations throughout the country. The government hoped to free Indians from federal supervision and to abolish the Bureau of Indian Affairs. Termination policy urged Indian tribes to manage their own affairs and to change their traditional institutions and culture to those of modern American society. Thus, it sought to put an end to schools, health clinics, and hospitals operated for Indians only as well as to tribal governments.

The U.S. government put this policy into action in Mississippi by establishing various vocational training programs to prepare the Choctaw for jobs off the reservation. Some Choctaw received training on the reservation, but others moved to Chicago, Cleveland, and Dallas to attend vocational training centers. Although many Choctaw participated in these programs and some moved to cities to seek employment once they had learned a trade, most preferred to remain on the reservation despite the government's efforts and the relative lack of jobs there.

In the 1960s, the administrations of Presidents John F. Kennedy and Lyndon B. Johnson concluded that the American Indian would be better served by a federal policy that encouraged self-determination, which would allow Indians to choose for themselves whether to remain on their reservations or to move to towns and cities where they would be more likely to adopt the culture of the American mainstream. During these administrations, Congress again passed various acts and programs to aid the economic and social development of Indians. The Indian Self-Determination and Education Assistance Act, passed in 1975, provided greater opportunity for Indians to participate in their own government and education. Indians were to direct and staff the federally funded programs and services available to them.

Since the introduction of the self-determination policy, the Choctaw on the Mississippi reservation have greatly improved their economy. To provide job opportunities for their people, Choctaw leaders established the Chata Development Company in 1969. The company has built or repaired numerous homes on the reservation and constructed several community centers and tribal offices. In 1973, it completed an industrial park at Pearl River, the largest Choctaw community in Mississippi. The park has attracted many industrial firms who have located their facilities on the reservation. In 1977, Chairman Phillip Martin was instrumental in persuading the Packard Electric Division of the General Motors Corporation to establish in Pearl River the Chata Wire Harness Enterprise, which employs many Choctaw to assemble electrical parts for some cars manufactured by the automobile company. Several other plants have opened in the park during the 1980s, including the Choctaw Greeting Enterprise of the American Greeting Corporation, where Choctaw workers assemble greeting cards, and the Choctaw Electronics Enterprise of the Oxford Investment Company of Chicago, where they manufacture automobile radio speakers. The many jobs for the Choctaw created by the firms in the industrial park have spurred recent efforts by the tribal leadership to seek companies willing to locate plants in the other nearby Choctaw communities. As a result, in 1986 new plants were opened in nearby DeKalb County and in the town of Carthage, near the Choctaw community of Redwater.

Of the approximately 1,000 persons who are now employed on the Choctaw reservation, most either work at these manufacturing plants or hold positions with various tribal agencies sponsored by the federal government. All but a few have abandoned farming as a way to earn a living. Although several hundred more Choctaw have jobs off the reservation, the unemployment rate among the tribespeople is slightly more than 20 percent, well above the national average. The average income of the Choctaw has risen in recent years, but it is still below that of citizens of Mississippi and of the United States.

The number of Choctaw living in Mississippi during the past several decades has also steadily increased. Between 1960 and 1980, the state's Choctaw population grew from 3,119 to 6,313. Independent surveys show that nearly 2,000 more Choctaw lived on or near the reservation during the early 1980s than did 2 decades ago. The reservation population in 1982 numbered 4,398, approximately 60 percent of whom were under 25 years of age.

Most of the children on the reservation attend elementary schools in their communities or the Choctaw Central High School, which was built in 1963 at Pearl River. Despite the efforts of these public schools, the educational level of the average Mississippi Choctaw is still low. Approximately 55 percent of the adult population has completed fewer than 8 years of schooling; 37 percent, between 8 and 12; and only 8 percent, more than 12. Although the majority of the Choctaw people now speak both Choctaw and English, a recent study indicated that only about 58 percent of the population can speak English well and only about 50 percent are skilled in writing the language. To combat these problems, the U.S. government has established adult education programs at Pearl River, which have helped many Choctaw to receive eighth-grade certificates and high school diplomas.

The Mississippi Choctaw are also working to provide better health care for their people. Infectious diseases, particularly pneumonia and tuberculo-

The Choctaw Greetings Enterprise, which employs many of the more than 4,000 tribespeople who live on the Mississippi reservation today.

sis, are the number-one cause of death among the Indians; therefore, their health-service programs aim to educate the Choctaw in preventive medicine, proper nutrition, and the elimination of environmental health hazards. The Choctaw Health Center, a 43-bed hospital, has aided this effort since it opened in 1976. Smaller health clinics are also in operation now in the Choctaw communities of Bogue Chitto, Conehatta, and Redwater.

The quality of housing for the Choctaw in Mississippi has improved throughout the 20th century. During the 1930s, about 200 small wood homes were built through a federal housing construction program. Very few additional new homes were constructed on the reservation until 1965, when the Choctaw Housing Authority was established. This organization has been responsible for the building of more than 200 houses, and many more are currently under construction or planned for the future. These brick homes have many of the same modern conveniences found in most homes throughout the country today.

The Choctaw presently on the reservation still have their own tribal government, although its structure is different from that organized in 1945. In 1975, the Choctaw adopted a revised constitution, which changed the title of chairman to chief and called for this official to be elected by the members of the entire tribe to a four-year term

(continued on page 94)

THE CHOCTAW LANGUAGE

Linguists, scholars who study the structure and evolution of human speech, have identified 221 different languages spoken by Indians in North America. These languages can be grouped into several linguistic families by similarities in their grammatical structures. Tribes in the same linguistic family do not necessarily live in the same region or share other cultural characteristics, but anthropologists believe that resemblances between the languages of two different groups indicate that their ancestors may have belonged to a single group that spoke an early form of these languages in prehistoric times.

The Choctaw language belongs to the Muskogean linguistic family, which also includes the languages of several tribes, such as the Creek and Chickasaw, that were the Choctaw's neighbors in both Mississippi and Indian Territory. Because the sounds of Muskogean languages are very similar to those of English, the Choctaw language can be represented with the Roman alphabet. This factor, combined with the Choctaw's thirst for education, made it easy for Choctaw adults and children to learn to read and write in their language. Within a generation after their removal, most Choctaw were literate.

For this reason, the first missionaries to establish schools among the Choctaw in Indian Territory were able to translate their religious and educational materials and print them in Choctaw. The missionary who was perhaps most responsible for the tribe's quick rate of literacy was Presbyterian minister Cyrus Byington. Byington translated many hymns, the New Testament, and most of the Old Testament into Choctaw and compiled the first grammar and dictionary in the language. Aided by the staff of the American Board of Commissioners for Foreign Missions, he also published a tremendous number of tracts in Choctaw, including lectures on morality, biographies of Christian Indians, and bible stories for children. In 1837 alone, his output totalled more than 576,000 pages of text.

Although classes in the Choctaw's schools were conducted in English, the Choctaw language, both written and spoken, remained an important means of communication, especially among adults, throughout the history of the Choctaw Nation. The many newspapers published in the Nation in the late 19th century all contained columns and news written in Choctaw, even though the papers were operated by and for the increasing population of non-Indians. To combat the bias of these publications, *Indian Citizen* was established in 1889. Owned by Choctaw citizens, it was exclusively devoted to the concerns of the tribe. Each issue included local news, editorials, and reports from Washington, as well as some lively gossip. For less-educated tribespeople who could not read English, *Indian Citizen* also translated into Choctaw and published all the treaties the Choctaw had made with the United States and all federal laws pertaining to the tribe.

Today many Choctaws speak both English and Choctaw. Their native language is preserved in the names of cities, towns, counties, and rivers throughout Mississippi and Oklahoma. The word *Oklahoma* itself is derived from the Choctaw words *okla*, "people," and *homma*, "red." The area was first called Oklahoma by Choctaw chief Allen Wright in 1866 when he was asked what he would name Indian Territory if the United States succeeded in organizing it under one Indian government.

Below is a list of other currently used place names that were adapted from Choctaw words, along with a key to their pronunciation and their original meaning.

PLACE NAME	PRONUNCIATION	MEANING
Bogue Chitto	bow guh chit tuh	big creek
Bogue Homa	bow guh hoe muh	red creek
Coahoma	kuh hoe muh	red wildcat
Conehatta	ko nuh hat uh	gray skunk
Escatawpa	es kuh taw puh	beaver dam
Homochitto	hoe muh chih tuh	big red
Itta Bena	it uh bee nuh	wood camp
Neshoba	nuh show buh	wolf
Noxubee	knock shuh bee	fishy smell
Ofahoma	oh fuh hoe muh	red dog
Okalona	oak uh loan uh	people got there
Okatibbee	oak uh tih bee	water fight
Panola	puh no luh	cotton
Shubuta	shoe boo tuh	snake
Shuqualak	shug uh lock	crawfish hole
Tchula	chew luh	fox
Yalabusha	yal luh buh shuh	tadpole

A chanter leads a gathering of Choctaw in an ancient tribal song.

(continued from page 91)

rather than appointed by the council for two years. The tribal council now meets on the second Tuesday in January, April, July, and October of each year to discuss tribal matters, although special meetings may be called by the chief. The Choctaw government has the right to establish its own laws and judicial system; therefore, Mississippi has no political power over the reservation. The federal government, however, is ultimately responsible for the protection of the Choctaw and their property from encroachment by the state and its citizens.

Although the Choctaw government in Oklahoma owns several tracts of land, they are not organized as a reservation. The council of the western branch of the Choctaw does have the power to make tribal laws, but the Oklahoma Choctaw also must adhere to the laws of the state. Their tribal government has played a tremendous role in the lives of the tribespeople in recent years. Just as self-determination has allowed their Mississippi kin to flourish, the policy has helped the Choctaw government in Durant, Oklahoma, to administer many programs and establish institutions to improve the health, education, and income of the more than 26,700 residents of the state that the council recognizes as having a "certified degree of Indian blood" (CDIB). Although CDIB Choctaw may be as little as 1/500 Indian, they are all registered as members of the tribe with the Choctaw government and therefore entitled to participate in the social programs it sponsors. Among the Oklahoma Choctaw council's recent projects have been the establishment of the Choctaw Housing Authority in Hugo, the Tallahina Indian Hospital in Tallahina, 3 Indian health clinics in Hugo, Broken Bow, and McAlester, and 5 community centers and 10 Headstart centers for the education of preschool children, which are located throughout southeastern Oklahoma.

The federal government contributes funds to many of these programs, and the Choctaw government provides additional financial support from the profits of several businesses operated by the council. Possibly the most successful of these is a large bingo parlor in Durant, which employs more than 150 people and attracts visitors from throughout Oklahoma and neighboring states. The Choctaw government also runs the Arrowhead Resort and Hotel in Canadian, Oklahoma, and has under construction the Choctaw Travel Center in Durant, which includes several stores for tourists and residents in the area.

The Choctaw in both Oklahoma and Mississippi have retained much of their cultural heritage. They continue to perform many of their ancient tribal songs and dances, and after centuries of play stickball and archery competitions remain popular. Some Choctaw women still weave baskets and make traditional clothing. Handmade Choctaw dresses, frequently worn by older women, require up to six yards of fabric for the skirt alone. Men's shirts for special occasions are usually decorated with intricate beadwork and trimmed with ribbon. Men also often wear ribboned belts and black felt hats.

The Choctaw's traditional customs and costumes are displayed every summer at the Mississippi Choctaw's Indian

A game of ishtaboli, one of the many traditional Choctaw activities still enjoyed by members of the tribe.

Fair, which they have held annually since 1949 to promote tourism. Each year more than 20,000 persons come to the campus of the Choctaw High School in Pearl River to attend the four-day event. Many leading national entertainers perform at the fair, helping to make it one of the most popular tourist attractions in the state of Mississippi. The Choctaw also convene in Tuskahoma, Oklahoma, every Labor Day for their annual festival. At both these events, many of the more than 45,000 CDIB Choctaw who today reside in Mississippi, Oklahoma, Louisiana, Alabama, Tennessee, Texas, California, and Washington gather to celebrate their common heritage. Together again, the Choctaw join in their traditional games and dances and share with the youngest members of the tribe their stories of the long-divided Choctaw people. ▲

BIBLIOGRAPHY

Baird, W. David. *The Choctaw People*. Phoenix, AZ: Indian Tribal Series, 1973.

Blanchard, Kendall. *The Mississippi Choctaw at Play: The Serious Side of Leisure*. Urbana: University of Illinois Press, 1981.

Bounds, Thelma V. *Children of Nanih Waiya*. San Antonio, TX: Naylor, 1964.

Debo, Angie. *The Rise and Fall of the Choctaw Republic*. 2nd ed. Norman: University of Oklahoma Press, 1961.

DeRosier, Arthur H., Jr. *The Removal of the Choctaw Indians*. Knoxville: University of Tennessee Press, 1970.

Foreman, Grant. *The Five Civilized Tribes*. Norman: University of Oklahoma Press, 1934.

Kidwell, Clara Sue, and Charles Roberts. *The Choctaws: A Critical Bibliography*. Bloomington: Indiana University Press for Newberry Library, 1980.

Lewis, Anna. *Chief Pushmataha, American Patriot: The Story of the Choctaws' Struggle for Survival*. New York: Exposition Press, 1959.

McKee, Jesse O., and Jon A. Schlenker. *The Choctaws: Cultural Evolution of a Native American Tribe*. Jackson: University Press of Mississippi, 1980.

Reeves, Carolyn Keller, ed. *The Choctaw Before Removal*. Jackson: University Press of Mississippi, 1985.

Wells, Samuel J., and Roseanna Tubby, eds. *After Removal: The Choctaw in Mississippi*. Jackson: University Press of Mississippi, 1986.

THE CHOCTAW AT A GLANCE

TRIBE *Choctaw*

CULTURE AREA *Southeast*

GEOGRAPHY *Gulf Coastal Plain*

LINGUISTIC FAMILY *Muskogean*

CURRENT POPULATION *13,621 in former Choctaw Nation in Oklahoma; 6,300 in State of Mississippi*

FIRST CONTACT *Hernando de Soto, Spanish, 1540*

FEDERAL STATUS *recognized in Oklahoma. Reservation in Mississippi*

GLOSSARY

agent A person appointed by the Bureau of Indian Affairs to supervise U.S. government programs on a reservation and/or in a specific region; after 1908 the title "superintendent" replaced "agent."

alikchi The Choctaw word for medicine man or shaman. This person was in charge of conducting ceremonies to assure the success of hunting or war parties for the tribe.

allotment U.S. policy, applied starting in 1887, to break up tribally owned reservations by assigning individual farms and ranches to Indians. Intended as much to discourage traditional communal activities as to encourage private farming and to assimilate Indians into mainstream American life.

annuity Compensation for land and/or resources based on terms of a treaty or other agreement between the United States and an individual tribe; consisted of goods, services, and cash given to the tribe every year for a specified period.

archaeology The recovery and study of evidence of human ways of life, especially that of prehistoric peoples but also including that of historic peoples.

artifact Any object made by human beings, such as a tool, garment, dwelling, or ornament.

Bureau of Indian Affairs (BIA) A U.S. government agency established by the War Department in 1824 and assigned to the Department of the Interior in 1849. Originally intended to manage trade and other relations with Indians, the BIA now seeks to develop and implement programs to encourage Indians to manage their own affairs and to improve their educational opportunities and general social and economic well-being.

Choctaw Indian tribe that traditionally lived in what is now Mississippi, western Alabama, and eastern Louisiana. Today, the Choctaw also live in Oklahoma, Tennessee, Texas, California, and Washington.

clan A multigenerational group having a shared identity, organization, and property, based on belief in their descent from a common ancestor. Because clan members consider themselves closely related, marriage within a clan is strictly prohibited.

culture The learned behavior of humans; nonbiological, socially taught activities; the way of life of a group of people.

Five Civilized Tribes A loose confederation of the Creek, Choctaw, Chickasaw, Cherokee, and Seminole tribes, formed in 1859 to preserve Indian self-government in the face of a growing number of non-Indian settlers in Indian Territory. The word "civilized" referred to the adoption by these tribes of many non-Indian customs.

floodplain Level land that is frequently submerged when rivers flood during the spring thaw. This flooding returns to the soil nutrients that are drained every year by cultivation.

Green Corn dance Celebration of purification, forgiveness, and thanksgiving held annually when the new crop of corn ripened.

Indian Reorganization Act (IRA) The 1934 federal law that ended the policy of allotting plots of land to individuals and provided for political and economic developments of reservation communities. The responsibilities of self-government were permitted, and tribes wrote their own constitutions for that purpose.

Indian Territory An area in the south central United States, including most of the present state of Oklahoma, in which the U.S. government wanted to resettle Indians from other regions, especially from states east of the Mississippi River.

matrilineal; matrilineality A principle of descent by which kinship is traced through female ancestors; the basis for Choctaw clan membership.

mingo A Choctaw district chief.

mound A large earthen construction built by prehistoric American Indians as a base for a public building or to contain human graves.

Nanih Waiya A large mound sacred to the Choctaw and looked upon as their birthplace. Also the name given to the first council house in the Choctaw Nation in Indian Territory.

nation A self-governing Indian group.

prehistory Anything that happened before written records existed for a given locality. In North America, anything earlier than the first contact with Europeans is considered to be prehistoric.

PICTURE CREDITS

JESSE O. McKEE is professor and chair of the department of geography and area development at the University of Southern Mississippi. He holds a B.S. degree in geography from Clarion University of Pennsylvania and an M.A. and Ph.D. in geography from Michigan State University. He is coauthor of *The Choctaws: Cultural Evolution of a Native American Tribe,* coeditor of *Mississippi: A Sense of Place,* and editor of *Ethnicity in Contemporary America: A Geographical Appraisal.* He has also authored several articles and book chapters on the Choctaw and various other topics in cultural geography. Among the many research grants Professor McKee has received are a Fulbright-Hays travel grant for geographic research in Cameroon and a Geographic Alliance grant from the National Geographic Society for the improvement of geographic education in public secondary schools.

FRANK W. PORTER III, General Editor of INDIANS OF NORTH AMERICA, is Director of the Chelsea House Foundation for American Indian Studies. He holds an M.A. and Ph.D. from the University of Maryland, where he also earned his B.A. He has done extensive research concerning the Indians of Maryland and Delaware and is the author of numerous articles on their history, archaeology, geography, and ethnography. He was formerly Director of the Maryland Commission on Indian Affairs and American Indian Research and Resource Institute, Gettysburg, Pennsylvania, and he has received grants from the Delaware Humanities Forum, the Maryland Committee for the Humanities, the Ford Foundation, and the National Endowment for the Humanities, among others.